SAINSBURY'S
COMPLETE
VEGETARIAN
COOKING

ROSAMOND RICHARDSON

SAINSBURY'S
COMPLETE VEGETARIAN COOKING

ROSAMOND RICHARDSON

Published exclusively for J Sainsbury plc
Stamford House
Stamford Street
London SE1 9LL
by Martin Books
Simon & Schuster Consumer Group
Grafton House
64 Maids Causeway
Cambridge CB5 8DD

First published 1991
Second impression 1992
ISBN 0 85941 686 0

Text and photographs © 1991, 1992. J Sainsbury plc

Design: Bridgewater Design
Photography: Tim Imrie
Styling: Anna Tait
Food Preparation: Mandy Wagstaff
Printed and bound in Italy by Printer Trento

NOTES

Ingredients are given in both metric and imperial measures.
Use either set of quantities but not a mixture of both in any
one recipe.

All spoon measurements are level:
1 tablespoon = one 15 ml spoon
1 teaspoon = one 5 ml spoon

Freshly ground black pepper is intended where pepper is
listed.

Fresh herbs are used unless otherwise stated. If unobtainable, dried
herbs can be substituted in cooked dishes but halve the quantities.

Eggs are size 3 unless otherwise stated.

PREPARATION AND COOKING TIMES

Preparation and cooking times are included as a general guide;
preparation times, especially, are approximate and timings are usually
rounded to the nearest 5 minutes.
Preparation times include the time taken to prepare ingredients in the
list, but not to make any 'basic' recipe.
The cooking times given at the heads of the recipes denote cooking
periods when the dish can be left largely unattended, e.g. baking,
stewing, and not the total amount of cooking for the recipe. Always read
and follow the timings given for the steps of the recipe in the method.

PREVIOUS PAGE (CLOCKWISE)
Nasturtium harlequin salad (PAGE 138)
Curried baby aubergines (PAGE 57)
Savoury cheese and vegetable clafoutis (PAGE 35)
Sesame pitta bread (PAGE 117)
Cucumber and cheese mousse (PAGE 33)
Watercress dip with green peppercorns (PAGE 25)
Mushroom butterflies (PAGE 45)
Farfalle with basil and courgettes (PAGE 87)

CONTENTS

A VEGETARIAN DIET

WHAT IS A VEGETARIAN?

A vegetarian is someone who eats only vegetables, fruits and grains, and any foods which are free from ingredients derived from the slaughter of animals. They avoid all meat, fish and poultry, and associated products such as gelatine, stock cubes and animal fats such as suet, dripping and lard, for which vegetarian substitutes are available.

There is considerable diversity among vegetarians concerning the intake of milk, cheese and eggs – and even honey. Vegans eat none of these, or any processed foods that use animal products, to ensure that no animal suffers to produce the food that they eat. The manufacture of the product must not involve testing on animals either. Thus their diet is of food from plant sources only.

There are many shades of vegetarianism, and many reasons for changing to a meatless diet. Some people change to a vegetarian diet because of food allergies; others because of a general feeling that it provides a healthier diet. Some may not be able to afford meat, or may prefer the flavours of vegetarian food. Self-styled 'demi veg' people may sometimes eat a little fish and chicken on social occasions to make life easier for their friends.

Butter is generally acceptable to vegetarians because the animal is not killed to obtain the product. Some margarines contain fish oils and whey: whey cannot ordinarily be made without using animal rennet, obtained from the stomach of a newly-killed calf. There are non-dairy margarines available which are acceptable to vegans, and also non-dairy ice creams.

Some vegetarians prefer to avoid products derived from factory-farmed cows, and opt for goat's milk and sheep's yogurt: both are delicious and commonly available. Likewise there is a wide variety of goat's and sheep's cheeses on the market, some of which do not contain animal rennet (see page 8).

Ice creams often contain animal fats and non-vegetarian emulsifiers, but vegetable-fat ice creams are available, as well as ice cream made from soya milk. Some prepared foods such as desserts, biscuits, soups, pastries and pizzas are not suitable for vegetarians, so the best advice is to read the labels to ensure that prepared foods are compatible with your vegetarian diet. Processed foods suitable for vegetarians are often highlighted with special flashes.

WHY VEGETARIAN?

People become vegetarians for a variety of reasons: they may take an ethical viewpoint, objecting to the idea of eating an animal that has been reared away from its natural environment merely to be killed as food. This objection is often linked to religious creeds, and certain religions extend the view to encompass the sanctity of all animal life. For others, economy may be a motivating factor: the shopping trolley of a vegetarian can be less expensive than that of a meat-eater. The economic argument goes beyond personal considerations: some vegetarians are concerned because producing meat as opposed to plant protein is much more costly in terms of land and crop resources: vast quantities of cereal crops, which could be used for human consumption, are used instead to feed these animals before they are slaughtered. Yet another reason for becoming vegetarian may be linked to health and fitness. A vegetarian diet incorporates many of the NACNE (National Advisory Committee on Nutrition Education) recommendations on food and health, including a reduced intake of saturated fats, salt and sugar, and an increased amount of fibre, as well as a reduced number of daily calories.

You may become vegetarian for any or none of these reasons: it may be that from pure preference, that of taste, you drop the meat from your diet and concentrate on all the other delicious foods that a vegetarian diet offers. Apart from the wonderful selection of local and exotic fruits and vegetables available, you can choose from pasta, nuts and seeds, rice, grains, pulses, cheese and egg dishes, curries and stir-fries to name but some. Dishes from many cultures can add colour and variety to your diet, including the cuisines of China, India, Indonesia, Italy, and Mexico.

A VEGETARIAN LIFESTYLE

MAKING THE TRANSITION

Though all this sounds a bit serious, it doesn't have to be. Attitude is all: it is possible to become a vegetarian without being heavily moralistic about it. You can simply look at it from a positive and practical angle: it is a delicious, cheap and healthy way of eating. Since becoming a vegetarian, I have certainly felt more vital and alive. It is also fun to learn another way of cooking, a challenge to explore new recipes and to try out dishes from other cultures.

Whatever your age, occupation or lifestyle, a change to a well-balanced vegetarian diet is a healthy choice. If you wish to lose weight, for example, you can slim and stay healthy following a vegetarian regime (page 13). Similarly, if you have to attend frequent business lunches or social functions, being a vegetarian need not pose a problem. Nowadays most restaurants and pubs include at least one vegetarian dish on their menus which makes eating out for vegetarians much easier than it used to be. Cooking for one need not be more problematical than cooking for a single meat-eater, particularly if you have a small freezer. In fact, in many ways cooking for the single vegetarian is easier than for the lone meat-eater. (page 14)

A vegetarian diet is safe for anyone to adopt, whatever their age. You need not worry if you are planning to become a vegetarian later in life – well-balanced vegetarian food will provide all the nutrients you need to maintain a healthy diet, and you may find the change of diet contributes to a greater sense of well-being. This principle applies equally to vegetarian children: so long as they eat a balanced and varied diet and the intake of the B_{12} and D vitamins are monitored (pages 9–12), parents need not worry that their offspring are lacking in essential nutrients. If the children are thriving and full of energy you can feel confident that they are not suffering from a nutritional deficiency. The eating habits of a lifetime are often formed in childhood and, by advocating a vegetarian diet that is naturally rich in fibre and low in fat, you may well be setting your child on the path to a lifetime's pattern of healthy eating.

One way of easing yourself towards becoming vegetarian is to adapt conventional recipes with which you are already familiar: make a shepherds pie, for example, either using pulses (page 105), or if you prefer, soya meat-substitutes. As you gain confidence, look at classic recipes such as soufflés, crêpes and pasta, then at curries and stir-fries – and try delicious gourmet sauces to add elegant touches to your meals. You will find that many of these are simple, quick and easy to prepare and result in inspired combinations which will also appeal to the non-vegetarian. The joy of cooking vegetarian food is that you can explore the full potential of herbs and spices, making dishes smell and taste quite wonderful.

THE TIME-MYTH

Certain myths die hard. One is that cooking vegetarian food is more time-consuming than cooking food for a conventional diet. This is a myth I am happy to explode. Vegetarian cooking can be a great boon for a modern, high-pressure lifestyle: what is time-consuming about preparing pasta dishes, cooking rice, making an omelette, or chopping a salad? The fact is that when you cook anything for the first time it takes longer than when you become practised at it.

For some vegetarian recipes there may be a shift in the time taken to prepare a dish: for example, it may take slightly longer to prepare but require less time to cook. There are some processes that do require thinking ahead, like soaking pulses: but this is hardly more time-consuming than taking a joint of meat out of the freezer and remembering to leave time for it to defrost. All food reflects the care and time taken in its preparation. Vegetarian food is no different from any other in this respect.

I have found, too, that there are fewer pans, baking trays and saucepans to wash up than accumulate, for example, when cooking a traditional roast dinner.

THE STORE CUPBOARD

Basic foodstuffs and culinary stand-bys play an important part in the transition from carnivore to vegetarian, so

8 | here are some ideas for items to include in your vegetarian store cupboard, fridge and freezer.

FOR THE LARDER

RICE basmati white and brown; Italian risotto; brown long- or short-grain; wild rice.

PASTA dried, all shapes, sizes and colours, including less obvious ones like buckwheat and wholewheat spaghetti.

FLOURS a choice of organic or unbleached, white or wholemeal, buckwheat flour and polenta (coarse corn meal). Polenta is used to make a thick porridge which, when cold, can be cut into slices and fried, and then layered with cheese, vegetables and herbs and baked.

PULSES dried or canned, e.g. aduki beans, haricots, black-eyed beans, butterbeans, flageolets, kidney beans, mung beans, chick-peas, lentils (red, green and brown), marrowfat peas, pinto beans, split peas.

You can sprout some of these pulses, as well as seeds, very successfully in a salad-sprouter. Add them to salads to make them more nutritious; try alfalfa, sunflower and fenugreek; mung, lentils and black-eyed beans.

NUTS almonds, brazils, cashews, coconut (desiccated or creamed), hazelnuts, walnuts, peanuts, macadamia, chestnuts, pecans, pine kernels, pistachios.

SEEDS sunflower, sesame, pumpkin, poppy, fennel, dill, alfalfa (for sprouting).

GRAINS bulgar wheat, couscous, millet, pearl barley, buckwheat, oats and oatmeal, maize (sweetcorn).

OILS olive, sunflower, groundnut, soya, walnut, grapeseed.

DRIED FRUITS raisins, sultanas, currants, figs, prunes, apricots, peaches, apples, dates.

HERBS AND SPICES keep all the spices that you can fit on to your shelf – they store indefinitely. Only some herbs, however, dry well, and even these do not keep for longer than a year. Keep bay, rosemary, sage, thyme, and a quantity of dried mixed herbs from Provence. Grow fresh herbs such as basil, parsley and coriander.

SOYA SUBSTITUTES TVP (soya-protein made to resemble meat, either in chunks or in the form of 'mince').

QUORN or mycoprotein, another meat substitute derived from plant sources, which is high in dietary fibre and contains no animal fats or cholesterol. It is a good source of protein and low in calories, and its light savoury taste blends into many dishes.

SOYA PRODUCTS soy sauce or tamari for seasoning savoury dishes; soya milk, sweetened, unsweetened or flavoured, is a useful substitute for dairy milk. Tofu, the soft white curd of the fermented soya bean, can be smoked or marinated, and used in both sweet and savoury dishes.

MISCELLANEOUS garam masala paste or powder; yeast extract; sea or vegetable salt; vegetable stock cubes; dried yeast; olives; arrowroot; agar-agar or gelozone; fructose (fruit sugar) if you prefer it.

FOR THE FREEZER AND FRIDGE

Whatever your lifestyle, it is useful to have a supply of convenience foods in the larder or freezer. Many of the frozen convenience foods available now cater to the vegetarian consumer, and you can always keep some prepared pasta dishes, flans, quiches, and vegetable dishes in the freezer for when you want an effortless meal.

In addition, use your freezer to stock some of the following stand-bys: breads (Granary, pitta, par-baked loaves and rolls); breadcrumbs (fresh wholemeal); burgers (vegetable); casseroles and stews (make twice the quantity and freeze half); crêpes and pancakes; flan cases; grated cheeses; nuts and seeds; pasta (fresh) and pasta sauces; pastries; pizzas and pizza bases; pulses (cooked); purées (vegetable); sauces; sausages (vegetarian); soups; stocks (freeze in ice-cube containers); whole spices and some herbs.

For the fridge, vegetable pies, pizzas and pasties are available for short-term storage, and for light meals there are vegetable dips, pâtés and terrines. Pesto sauce keeps for a few weeks and is great for instant pasta dishes. A wide range of cheeses are available to vegetarians, and these are worth considering to clarify any confusion.

Cheeses made without animal rennet (page 6) are acceptable to vegetarians. Parmesan is made with animal rennet, so you can use vegetarian Cheddar as an alternative to this if you prefer. There are numerous other cheeses besides Cheddar made with vegetable rennet, which are preferred by some vegetarians: the information will be on the label. Many of the soft cheeses such as cottage cheese, cream cheese, mozzarella and Danish blue are suitable for vegetarians. Many excellent goat and sheep cheeses are available, such as goat 'logs', some of which are made with herbs. Feta and Roquefort are made with sheep's milk. Some of these are vegetarian. Gruyère, Camembert and Stilton are not vegetarian, but a vegetarian alternative can be used instead of these.

A NUTRITIONAL BALANCE

The secret of a healthy diet is variety: don't eat the same few dishes day after day. Eat foods that are fresh and wholesome and plenty of fresh vegetables and salads, balancing them with cereals and a few nuts and pulses. Add some fruit and dairy produce, and you can't go wrong. The vegetarian diet is rich in vitamins and minerals, high in fibre and, providing it is not too high in dairy produce, is low in saturated fats. In the right balance it is a healthy and nourishing way of eating.

PROTEIN

Protein is essential for healthy growth and repair of the body's cells. The first question that many people ask about the vegetarian diet is, 'How do you get your protein?' The answer is: from four main groups of protein-rich food:

PULSES e.g. lentils, beans, soya bean products such as soya milk, soya flour and tofu, as well as mycoprotein and textured vegetable protein or TVP (page 8)

GRAINS e.g. rice, pasta, cereals

NUTS AND SEEDS e.g. almonds, brazil nuts, peanuts; sunflower seeds, sesame seeds

DAIRY e.g. cheese, eggs, milk

It is important in order to maximise the body's benefit from its protein intake that these groups of protein-rich foods should be balanced in the vegetarian diet. This mixing of proteins is not complicated – the simplest way to do it is to include complementary proteins in one meal, and this is in fact the normal human way of eating. For example, eat beans on toast (pulse and grain), macaroni cheese (grain and dairy), muesli with yogurt (grain and dairy), dhal and rice (pulse and grain), hummus (pulse and seed), lentil nut roast (pulse and nuts), and rice pudding (grain and dairy).

You will easily get your daily protein requirement on a well-balanced vegetarian diet, whether you are very young, a teenager or elderly, so long as you include moderate amounts of these products regularly in your diet. There is an equivalent amount of protein in a simple meal of spaghetti with grated cheese, for example, as in an average helping of lamb or chicken.

CARBOHYDRATES

Carbohydrates provide our main source of energy, and they are normally provided by plant foods. The healthiest ones are unrefined, such as cereals – wholemeal bread, brown rice, pasta, oats, barley, millet, buckwheat and rye. Root vegetables – potatoes, parsnips, turnips and swedes – are also useful sources.

FATS AND OILS

Saturated fats, generally to be found in meat, meat products and some dairy products, are solid at room temperature (e.g. butter, lard). Palm oil and coconut oil are the only saturated fats from vegetable sources. One of the advantages of a vegetarian diet is that it is low in saturated fats which are generally agreed to be bad for the body's system as they are thought to cause high cholesterol levels in the blood: a common factor in heart disease.

Both monounsaturated and polyunsaturated fats are generally agreed to be better for the system and are thought not to have an adverse effect on the level of cholesterol in the blood. Olive oil is a monounsaturated fat. Nuts are very high in unsaturated fats as well as being high in fibre and rich in vital nutrients such as carbohydrates, vitamins and minerals. Sunflower, safflower, groundnut and soya oil are all high in polyunsaturated fats.

VITAMINS

A This is required for healthy skin, hair, nails, mucous membranes, and for resistance to infection. Found in, among other foodstuffs: red or yellow vegetables (carrots, tomatoes), leafy green vegetables, apricots. It is added to most margarines.

B The vitamins in the B group are needed for functions connected with the nervous system, the red blood cells, the utilisation of energy from food, etc. All the B vitamins except B_{12} occur in yeast and whole cereals.

B_1 peas, beans, potatoes and many other vegetables. Oranges, brazil nuts, sunflower seeds, wheatgerm.

B_2 dairy produce, mushrooms, almonds and hazelnuts.

B_3 dairy produce, peas, cereals, mushrooms.

B_6 green vegetables, dried fruits, sunflower seeds, pulses.

B_{12} not found in plant foods except for possibly some seaweeds. Only tiny amounts are needed and these are provided by dairy products. Vegans must include a B_{12} supplement or eat some foods fortified with B_{12} at least three times a week – e.g. some yeast extracts and spreads, vegetable protein mixes, soya milk and some other soya products, breakfast cereals, and so on: read the label! The elderly should take a vitamin B_{12} supplement.

C This is needed to fight infections and to speed the repair of the tissues. Found in fresh fruit, salad vege-tables, leafy green vegetables such as spinach and cabbage, peppers, tomatoes, potatoes.

D Vitamin D is essential in enabling the body to absorb calcium for strong bones and teeth. Found in: eggs, butter and margarine. Not found in plant foods. During expo-sure to sunlight the body manufactures its own vitamin D. The very young, the very old and those confined in-doors would be wise to take a vitamin D supplement.

E Required for the suppleness of the tissues. Found in: vegetable oil, cereals, eggs, nuts and seeds.

K This plays an essential role in blood clotting and the body's utilisation of proteins. Found in: vegetables and cereals.

MINERALS

CALCIUM

This is essential for healthy bones and teeth. It is found in: cheese and other dairy products, leafy green vege-tables, bread, hard water, nuts and seeds, dried fruits. Vitamin D aids the absorption of calcium.

IRON

It is needed for the body's manufacture of red blood cells. It is found in: leafy green vegetables, wholemeal bread, molasses, eggs, dried fruits (especially apricots), beans, seeds, pulses, nuts, chocolate and cocoa. A good intake of vitamin C aids the absorption of iron. Tea reduces the absorption of iron, so it is advisable to wait for about an hour after a meal before drinking tea.

MAGNESIUM

Needed to enable the body to utilise carbohydrates. It is found in: green vegetables, bread, milk, peas.

PHOSPHORUS

An important trace element found in nearly all foods, vegetables, bread, milk.

POTASSIUM AND SODIUM

Found in nearly all foods.

ZINC

Essential for a number of functions concerned with heal-ing, reproduction and metabolism. Found in: sesame seeds, cheese, almonds, lentils, haricot beans, whole-meal bread, brown rice. Freezing reduces the level of zinc in foods.

VEGETARIAN SLIMMING

Vegetarian food lends itself naturally to a slimming regime. It focuses the attention on a way of eating, and this is a great aid to maintaining the willpower necessary for successful dieting. Another of its advantages is that you can fill up on vegetables and salads, satisfying your hunger pangs while keeping your daily calorie intake low. Being careful to cut down on dairy products such as butter and cream, and not overdoing your intake of nuts, you can enjoy a diet of widely diverse foods and flavours while losing weight.

There are many wonderful foods to choose from apart from the colourful array of fruit and vegetables on the shop shelves: pasta and rice are excellent staples, pulses are satisfying and nutritious, you can eat eggs and cheese in moderation, and the various grains and seeds add interest and texture to meals of all kinds. You have to relinquish puddings, cakes and biscuits, of course, as on all diets, but at hungry moments you can fill up with raw vegetables such as radishes, cucumber, carrots and celery; or fruit, especially grapes, and soft fruits in summer. Dried fruits are also an excellent, nutritious source of energy at low moments, so have a stock of apricots or sun-dried raisins to hand to tide you over lapses of willpower.

As in all dieting, the important thing is balance. You must ensure that you get the requisite amount of vitamins and minerals, fats and oils, protein, carbohydrates and dietary fibre to keep the body healthy while it loses its excess weight. So work out your daily calorie requirement taking these factors into consideration, following the guide-lines on pages 9–12. Avoid alcohol and drink instead lots of mineral water: anything from one to two litres per day. This not only helps to keep the stomach feeling full, but it also flushes the system clean. Take plenty of exercise: increase the amount of walking that you do, or take up a sport. And try some herb teas – they come in lovely flavours like lemon and lime, mixed fruit, lime flower and mint, strawberry, rosehip and peppermint, to name but some. If you drink a lot of ordinary tea and coffee, the caffeine content reduces the body's capacity to absorb vitamins.

A friend of mine who used to be very tubby slimmed down following an uncomplicated vegetarian regime until I hardly recognised him in the street – he was a completely different shape with his new sleek and healthy look. He told me that not only had he steadfastly nibbled his crudités and fresh fruit when hungry, but at mealtimes he had simply eaten *half* the quantity he usually ate and the weight had dropped off him.

With these guide-lines in mind, you too can slim down by following a light vegetarian regime. For example, for breakfast have a grated apple mixed with thick yogurt and a sprinkling of muesli, and some herb tea. For lunch, soup is excellent because it is quite filling but not too rich; have pitta bread and a little hummus to follow, and a small tossed salad. At teatime, more herb tea and some fresh fruit. Make supper your main meal, cooking a well-balanced vegetarian dish, and eating half your usual quantity. Make a mixed salad with tofu sliced into it, sprinkle it with pumpkin seeds or sunflower seeds, and toss it in an interesting dressing. End the meal with fresh fruit or a sorbet or fruit salad. Later on in the evening, if you feel peckish, make a soothing herb tea such as chamomile, and keep nibbling fresh fruit. On this kind of daily diet you won't feel hungry at all, and the unwanted weight will dissolve away.

THE SOCIABLE VEGETARIAN

Several questions may remain for those planning to become vegetarians. How do you become a vegetarian and remain sociably acceptable? What if you are the only member of a meat-eating family who wants to become vegetarian? If you live on your own, how easy is it to cook vegetarian food for one? How do you feed a vegetarian friend if you yourself are a meat-eater? What about eating out in restaurants? Or – even more difficult – in friends' houses?

Perhaps your meat-eating friends feel inadequate at the thought of having to meet your needs; or feel unable to respect your choices. A relaxed, cheerful attitude will usually disarm them more effectively than a defensive or moralistic reply. It pays to stress the positive aspects: how delicious the diet is, how much cheaper, how much better you feel, how simple many of the recipes are – indeed, how some of them, like pasta dishes and stir-fries, are in the common repertoire. I have frequently found that people's minds go blank at the thought of what to cook for a vegetarian visitor: so emphasise this common bank: the curries, the egg and cheese dishes that they will know how to cook, the sauces, salads, and rice dishes.

Another kind of problem arises when you are the only member of a family who wants to turn vegetarian. Inevitably this is going to make more work for the cook-in-charge if he or she is going to have to cook two meals every time you eat together. So, again, look for the traditional recipes that are meatless: pasta pesto, macaroni cheese, or soufflés; a risotto or pizza, or stuffed baked potatoes to name but a few. You can try out TVP on them too and see if they notice the difference! Over a short time a new pattern of eating will emerge – a compromise, inevitably, but not a crushing burden for the cook.

Cooking for one on a vegetarian diet presents the same problems as for the solo meat-eater: getting enough variety and interest in your daily intake, buying fresh foods in small quantities, and cooking small amounts at a time. But many of the recipes in this book freeze very well, so you can eat half and freeze the other half for another day. Salads are a great stand-by if you are eating alone: you can make them very nutritious by adding sprouted seeds, or slicing cheese or tofu into them. Add some chopped steamed vegetables, and dress the salad in an oriental dressing (page 130) that contains some protein in the form of beans. Soups, too, are quick to prepare and very nutritious. They are an excellent stand-by for everyday meals, and they also freeze very well.

My experience is that you can win friends over quite easily to your vegetarian meals – even the most confirmed carnivores. With a little care you can make a vegetarian lunch or dinner party look, smell and taste wonderful. If you use inspired combinations and elegant sauces, your guests will hardly notice that they are eating a meal without meat. I have had a lot of fun feeding friends since I became vegetarian, without wishing or needing to convert them all: after all, if I want them to respect my choices I can only respect theirs! So these occasions have been relaxed and cheerful, and the food has never let me down.

If, on the other hand, you are invited to a friend's house for a meal, it is helpful to have a word with them about your diet; they may welcome a few ideas for vegetarian recipes which are easy to prepare. Certainly, if you are dining with people you don't know well, you owe it to them to let them know in advance that you are vegetarian. On one or two occasions I have been in an embarrassing situation where the hostess didn't know that I was vegetarian, and I was faced with the choice of pushing my food to the side of the plate, or taking the attitude, 'when in Rome do as the Romans do'. I do feel that it is actually very rude to refuse someone's food, whatever your scruples. They have prepared it with care and thought, for you, and it is a rejection of more than the food itself. To do so verges on the self-righteous, particularly if you have not been vegetarian all your life. So, unless you *are* prepared to eat anything that is put in front of you, it is best to make your situation clear from the beginning, for their sake as well as yours.

The same applies to eating out in restaurants: if you are booking ahead, always let the chef know that you want a vegetarian meal. A good chef will welcome it as he can then give rein to his creativity and try out a speciality for you. If that is not his attitude then you have chosen the wrong place, and he has lost a customer! If you are eating out without booking, it is always worth telling the waiter, since there may well be a vegetarian option which is not prominently billed. Generally speaking, eating places are getting the message that vegetarianism is more common – and acceptable – than it used to be. You are no longer in a small minority.

Once again, attitude plays a part. I have had the experience of eating out with someone who was very self-righteous about being vegetarian, and who argued with the waiter and even the manager about the finer points, making everyone around feel very uncomfortable. I don't feel that is necessary, nor does it give vegetarians a good reputation. A restaurant is the wrong time and place to have moral arguments. If it is true that you are what you eat, then it is also true that your attitude to food speaks volumes. If you are not prepared to be flexible then it is better to eat only at places that offer purely vegetarian or vegan food.

There are many shades of vegetarianism, and many reasons for changing to a meatless diet. Undoubtedly there is a huge public interest in the vegetarian lifestyle, it has a more popular image than ever before, and engenders genuine interest among the young and even the very young. I shall never forget my little niece saying to me, when she was only five years old: 'Animals are my friends and I don't eat my friends'. Sublime simplicity: out of the mouths of babes . . .

For further information you can write to The Vegetarian Society at either of these addresses:

53 Marloes Road
Kensington
London W8 6LA
Telephone: 071-937 7739

Parkdale
Dunham Road
Altrincham
Cheshire WA14 4QG
Telephone: 061-928 1793

CHAPTER ONE

SOUPS AND DIPS

COURGETTE AND LEEK SOUP WITH BRIE

SERVES 4–6

50 g (2 oz) butter or margarine
• • •
625 g (1¼ lb) courgettes, sliced
• • •
250 g (8 oz) leeks, sliced
• • •
900 ml (1½ pints) vegetable stock
• • •
3 tablespoons single cream
• • •
2 tablespoons chopped parsley
• • •
75 g (3 oz) ripe Brie or soft goat cheese
• • •
salt and pepper to taste
• • •

PREPARATION AND COOKING TIME: 30–35 MINUTES

The delicate flavour of courgettes in this soup is sharpened with the pungent taste of leeks, and the addition of a little cream blends them perfectly. Float slices of cheese on top, and bubble them under the grill for a mouth-watering finishing touch.

Melt the butter or margarine in a large saucepan, add the courgettes and leeks, and cook gently, stirring frequently until they are coated with the fat. Cover the pan and cook over a medium heat for 5 minutes, stirring occasionally. Do not allow the vegetables to brown. Add the stock and bring to the boil. Cover the pan and simmer over a gentle heat for 15–20 minutes until the vegetables are tender.

Blend smoothly, and season to taste with salt and pepper, then return the soup to the pan. Stir in the cream and parsley and reheat gently. Ladle into heatproof bowls.

Slice the cheese thinly and float a few slices in each bowl. Place the bowls under a hot grill for a few moments before serving so that the cheese melts a little.

Sage bread (PAGE 122)
Fennel soup with ginger and garlic
Soupe à l'oignon gratinée
Vichyssoise
Courgette and leek soup with Brie

FENNEL SOUP WITH GINGER AND GARLIC

SERVES 4

1 tablespoon sesame oil

· · ·

6 large garlic cloves, sliced

· · ·

2 medium-size heads of fennel, chopped

· · ·

25 g (1 oz) root ginger, peeled and grated finely

· · ·

900 ml (1½ pints) vegetable stock

· · ·

soy sauce to taste

· · ·

5 tablespoons single cream (optional)

· · ·

PREPARATION TIME: 20 MINUTES + 25 MINUTES COOKING

This soup is one of my personal favourites. I love fennel, whether cooked or uncooked, and the ginger gives the soup a distinctively spicy quality. It makes a delicious lunch served with fresh Granary bread, or you can serve it as an elegant first course for a supper party.

Heat the oil in a large saucepan, add the garlic, and sauté very gently for 4–5 minutes, stirring frequently until softened. Add the fennel and stir for about 10 minutes until it begins to soften. Add the ginger and stock and bring to a gentle simmer. Cook, partially covered, for about 25 minutes.

Allow the soup to cool slightly, and then liquidise and strain it. Season to taste with soy sauce. Stir in the cream if used.

SOUPE À L'OIGNON GRATINÉE

SERVES 4

50 g (2 oz) butter or margarine

· · ·

625 g (1¼ lb) onions, sliced very finely

· · ·

600 ml (1 pint) vegetable stock

· · ·

8 slices of french bread

· · ·

75 g (3 oz) vegetarian Cheddar cheese, grated

· · ·

salt, pepper and grated nutmeg

· · ·

PREPARATION TIME: 10 MINUTES + ABOUT 40 MINUTES COOKING

The taste of this soup always reminds me of Paris, where I once spent many happy weeks staying near the famous Les Halles market – now transformed into a stunning shopping centre. The traditional onion soup of the market-men did not, however, disappear with them: it is still to be found there. Here is my version of it.

In a heavy-bottomed saucepan, and over a low heat, melt the butter or margarine, add the onions, and sauté very gently, stirring constantly, for about 5 minutes, or until well coated with the fat. Lower the heat and cover the pan tightly. Cook very gently for 20 minutes, stirring occasionally, until the onions are soft and sweet but not brown.

Pour in the stock and simmer for a further 10 minutes. Season to taste with salt, pepper and nutmeg, and ladle the soup into individual heatproof soup bowls. Cover the slices of bread with the cheese and float them in the soup. Place the bowls under a very hot grill for a minute or two until the cheese forms a golden bubbling crust on top.

BLENDER BROCCOLI SOUP

SERVES 4–6

750 g (1½ lb) broccoli

· · ·

900 ml (1½ pints) vegetable stock

· · ·

1 tablespoon dried mixed herbs

· · ·

250 g (8 oz) crème fraîche or soured cream

· · ·

salt and pepper, if necessary

· · ·

PREPARATION AND COOKING TIME: 20–25 MINUTES

Quick and simple to prepare, this is a fabulous soup. Serve it with warm sesame rolls or Thyme Oatcakes (page 124) and it makes a delicious starter to any meal, or a simple supper dish in its own right.

Steam the broccoli for 5–7 minutes, or until tender. Liquidise the broccoli with the stock and herbs until the mixture is smooth. Stir in the cream. Season to taste, heat through to just below boiling point, and serve at once.

VICHYSSOISE

> SERVES 4–6

50 g (2 oz) butter or margarine
· · ·
375 g (12 oz) leeks, sliced
· · ·
375 g (12 oz) potatoes, peeled and diced
· · ·
900 ml (1½ pints) vegetable stock
· · ·
4 tablespoons crème fraîche or soured cream
· · ·
salt and pepper to taste
· · ·
2 tablespoons chopped chives, to garnish
· · ·

PREPARATION TIME: 15 MINUTES + 45–50 MINUTES COOKING + CHILLING

Smooth and pale green, this wonderful soup has delighted the palate ever since it was first produced by an unknown but inspired French chef. Serve it with Melba toast or bread-sticks.

In a large heavy-bottomed saucepan, melt the butter or margarine, add the leeks, and cook gently for about 10 minutes, stirring frequently until they are soft. Add the potatoes and stir for a further 5 minutes. Pour in the stock and simmer for 30–35 minutes until the vegetables are very soft.

Blend smoothly, and season to taste with salt and pepper. Chill the soup; when cold, stir in the cream. Serve chilled, sprinkled with the chopped chives.

GARLIC SESAME CROÛTONS

> SERVES 6–8

2 egg whites
· · ·
2 large garlic cloves, crushed
· · ·
4 teaspoons sesame seeds
· · ·
4 teaspoons soy sauce
· · ·
4 slices of day-old wholemeal bread, cut into small cubes
· · ·
sunflower oil for frying
· · ·

PREPARATION AND COOKING TIME: 10 MINUTES

Whisk the egg whites stiffly and fold in the garlic, sesame seeds and soy sauce. Stir well. Fold the bread cubes into the mixture until they are evenly coated. Heat the oil in a saucepan, add the bread and fry until the croûtons are crisp and golden all over. Drain on kitchen paper and serve as soon as possible.

RUSSIAN BORSCHT

> SERVES 4

3 tablespoons sunflower oil
· · ·
1 very large uncooked beetroot, peeled and grated finely
· · ·
1 small onion, chopped finely
· · ·
6 celery sticks, sliced thinly
· · ·
900 ml (1½ pints) vegetable stock
· · ·
a pinch of sugar
· · ·
salt and pepper to taste
· · ·
To garnish:
4 tablespoons soured cream or yogurt
2 tablespoons chopped chervil
· · ·

PREPARATION TIME: 20 MINUTES + 20–25 MINUTES COOKING

This famous soup originated in Russia and eastern Europe and is suitably warming for cold climates. The original recipe contains beef stock, but here is my vegetarian version which is still rich, tasty and filling. It is delicious served with oatcakes or warm wholemeal bread and butter.

In a heavy-bottomed saucepan, heat the oil, add all the vegetables, and cook gently for about 8–10 minutes, stirring frequently. Add the stock and bring to simmering point. Add the sugar, and season to taste with salt and pepper. Cook, partially covered, for 15–20 minutes.

Check the seasoning, and pour the soup into four bowls. Float 1 tablespoon of soured cream or yogurt in the centre of each helping, and serve sprinkled with the chopped chervil.

AVOCADO AND CHERVIL SOUP

SERVES 2

40 g (1½ oz) butter or margarine
· · ·
4 tablespoons finely chopped chervil
· · ·
1 large ripe avocado, peeled and stoned
· · ·
450 ml (¾ pint) vegetable stock
· · ·
284 ml (½ pint) carton of single cream or milk
· · ·
salt and pepper to taste
· · ·
PREPARATION TIME: 15 MINUTES + CHILLING

The delicate flavour of chervil is quite individual, and it goes beautifully with the pleasantly bland flavour of ripe avocado.

Melt the butter or margarine in a saucepan, add the chervil, and cook gently for 5 minutes. Mash the avocado flesh and liquidise it with the stock. Add the cream or milk, stir in the herb mixture, and season to taste with salt and pepper. Chill the soup before serving.

PUMPKIN SOUP WITH GARLIC SESAME CROÛTONS

SERVES 6

50 g (2 oz) butter or margarine
· · ·
1 kg (2 lb) pumpkin, peeled, de-seeded and diced
· · ·
2 onions, sliced finely
· · ·
4 large tomatoes, peeled and quartered
· · ·
1.5 litres (2½ pints) vegetable stock
· · ·
125 ml (4 fl oz) double cream or crème fraîche
· · ·
salt and pepper to taste
· · ·
Garlic Sesame Croûtons (page 19), to garnish
· · ·
PREPARATION TIME: 25 MINUTES + 30–40 MINUTES COOKING

In October great piles of golden pumpkins appear in greengrocers' shops, ready for Hallowe'en – or for pumpkin soup. This version, with tomatoes, is delicious with warmed french bread.

Melt the butter or margarine in a large saucepan, add the pumpkin and the onions, and cook gently, stirring frequently until they are coated with the fat. Add the tomatoes and stir over a medium heat for a further 5 minutes. Pour in the stock and bring to the boil. Cover the pan and simmer over a low heat for 20–30 minutes or until the vegetables are completely tender. Season to taste with salt and pepper.

Purée the mixture and return it to the pan. Stir in the cream or crème fraîche, and heat through. Serve with the garlic sesame croûtons.

Russian borscht
Pumpkin soup with garlic sesame croûtons
Irish soda bread (PAGE 122)
Blender broccoli soup

TOMATO AND TARRAGON SOUP

SERVES 4

50 g (2 oz) butter or margarine
• • •
1 large onion, chopped
• • •
12 medium-size tomatoes, skinned and chopped
• • •
2 tablespoons chopped tarragon, or 1 tablespoon dried tarragon
• • •
600 ml (1 pint) vegetable stock
• • •
5 tablespoons single cream
• • •
salt and pepper to taste
• • •
chopped tarragon, to garnish
• • •

PREPARATION AND COOKING TIME: 30 MINUTES

I n the height of summer, bring together the taste of tarragon with ever-plentiful tomatoes to make a really delicious hot-weather soup, which can be served chilled if you like, with warm garlic bread.

Melt the butter or margarine in a saucepan, add the onion and cook gently for 5–10 minutes until soft. Add the tomatoes and tarragon and cook for a further 2 minutes. Then add the stock and simmer gently for 10 minutes. Liquidise the soup, and then stir in the cream and season to taste with salt and pepper. Heat through and serve sprinkled with chopped tarragon.

CREAM OF PARSLEY SOUP

SERVES 4

40 g (1½ oz) butter or margarine
• • •
1 large onion, chopped finely
• • •
375 g (12 oz) potatoes, peeled and diced
• • •
600 ml (1 pint) vegetable stock
• • •
3–4 tablespoons finely chopped parsley
• • •
142 ml (5 fl oz) carton of single cream
• • •
salt to taste
• • •
4 parsley sprigs, to garnish
• • •

PREPARATION AND COOKING TIME: 50 MINUTES

N ot the most aromatic of herbs, parsley has, nonetheless, a forthright flavour, and is full of good things like iron and vitamins. Serve this soup with warm wholemeal rolls.

Melt the butter or margarine in a saucepan, add the onion, and fry gently for 5–10 minutes until soft, and then stir in the potatoes. Pour in the stock and simmer for 20–25 minutes, or until the potatoes are soft. Add the parsley, simmer for a few more minutes and then liquidise the soup. Add the cream and season to taste with salt. Heat through and serve with a sprig of parsley floating in the centre of each bowl.

PREVIOUS PAGE (CLOCKWISE)
Tomato and tarragon soup
Cream of parsley soup
Skordalia
Thyme oatcakes (PAGE 124)
Creamy avocado and spinach dip
Avocado and chervil soup
Creamy butterbean dip with herbs

CREAMY BUTTERBEAN DIP WITH HERBS

> SERVES 4–6

220 g (7½ oz) can of butterbeans, drained
· · ·
4 tablespoons natural yogurt
· · ·
2 garlic cloves, crushed
· · ·
1 tablespoon mayonnaise
· · ·
*a small bunch of herbs such as dill, basil, tarragon, chives,
chopped finely*
· · ·
2 teaspoons dried thyme
· · ·
salt and pepper to taste
· · ·
chopped parsley, to garnish
· · ·

PREPARATION TIME: 5 MINUTES

*This is especially simple to make if you have a food processor. The dip
is excellent with dry toast or cheese biscuits, and I often add a plateful
of carrot and celery sticks too.*

Blend together all the ingredients until they are thoroughly
mixed and of a lovely creamy consistency. Put the dip into a
serving bowl, cover it with clingfilm and chill. Sprinkle with
the chopped parsley before serving.

WATERCRESS DIP WITH GREEN PEPPERCORNS

> SERVES 6–8

2 bunches of watercress, trimmed
· · ·
1 teaspoon dried green peppercorns, crushed
· · ·
175 g (6 oz) fromage blanc or fromage frais
· · ·
75 g (3 oz) mayonnaise
· · ·
25 g (1 oz) shelled walnuts, chopped finely
· · ·

PREPARATION TIME: 20 MINUTES + CHILLING

*The unique flavour of watercress permeates the fromage blanc or
fromage frais in this sublime dip, which turns a stunning green colour
in its preparation. Serve it with strips of pitta bread and a variety of
crudités such as raw cauliflower florets, tiny raw button mushrooms,
cucumber slices, and strips of yellow pepper.*

Blend the watercress smoothly with the peppercorns, fromage
blanc or fromage frais and mayonnaise. Put the dip into a
serving dish, cover with clingfilm, and chill until ready to
serve. Sprinkle with the chopped walnuts just before serving.

PICTURED ON TITLE PAGE

AUBERGINE AND PIMIENTO DIP

> SERVES 4–6

1 large aubergine
· · ·
6 tablespoons olive oil
· · ·
1 medium-size onion, chopped
· · ·
½ × 397 g (14 oz) can of pimientos, drained
· · ·
lemon juice to taste
· · ·
1–2 garlic cloves, crushed
· · ·
salt and pepper to taste
· · ·

PREPARATION TIME: 15 MINUTES + 30–40 MINUTES COOKING + CHILLING

*This dip has a mouth-wateringly soft texture, and the balance of
flavours is superb. The subtle taste of aubergine and the pungency of
pimientos are both highlighted by a touch of garlic. Serve this dip with
fingers of toast, or bread-sticks.*

Preheat the oven to Gas Mark 5/190°C/375°F. Place the
aubergine in a baking dish and bake for 30–40 minutes until
it is quite soft, and then allow it to cool.

Meanwhile heat half the oil in a saucepan, add the onion,
and sauté until it is soft. Scoop the flesh out of the aubergine
and mix it with the softened onion. Liquidise the mixture to a
purée with the remaining oil, the pimientos, lemon juice and
garlic. Season to taste with salt and pepper, and then chill the
dip before serving.

CREAMY AVOCADO AND SPINACH DIP

SERVES 6

250 g (8 oz) spinach
. . .
1 large avocado, stoned
. . .
125 g (4 oz) fromage frais
. . .
1 large garlic clove, crushed
. . .
2 tablespoons lemon juice
. . .
4 spring onions, chopped finely
. . .
salt and paprika to taste
. . .
PREPARATION TIME: 10 MINUTES

The addition of spinach to this creamy avocado mixture turns it a rich green colour and gives it a distinctive taste. Serve the dip with bread-sticks and a selection of crudités – carrots, cucumber, celery and cauliflower, for example.

Lightly cook the spinach in boiling water for about 5–7 minutes; drain and then squeeze out any excess water before chopping it. Scoop the flesh out of the avocado and blend it smoothly with the spinach and the fromage frais. Then mix in the garlic and lemon juice and stir in the spring onions. Season to taste with salt and paprika. Put the dip into a bowl, cover with clingfilm, and chill until ready to serve.

LEBANESE HUMMUS

SERVES 6–8

250 g (8 oz) dried chick-peas, soaked overnight, or 432 g (15 oz) can chick-peas
. . .
1 tablespoon tahina paste
. . .
juice of 1/2 lemon
. . .
3 tablespoons olive oil
. . .
4 tablespoons natural yogurt
. . .
2 garlic cloves, crushed
. . .
salt and pepper, if necessary
. . .
very finely chopped mint, to garnish
. . .
PREPARATION TIME: 10 MINUTES + SOAKING OVERNIGHT + 45 MINUTES COOKING

I was given this version of hummus at a Lebanese restaurant, and the owner was kind enough to share his secret. A little natural yogurt, and a finishing touch of finely chopped mint were what made all the difference to this traditional Middle-Eastern dish. Serve it with Sesame Pitta Bread (page 117) and a mixture of crisp crudités.

Drain the dried chick-peas and put them into a saucepan. Cover them with cold water, bring to the boil and simmer for 40–45 minutes, or until they are completely soft. Drain the cooked or canned chick-peas, reserving some of the liquid. Mix the chick-peas with all the remaining ingredients and blend them to a purée, adding a little of the chick-pea liquid if necessary to thin out the hummus. Season to taste with salt and pepper and turn out into a serving dish. Sprinkle with chopped mint just before serving.

GARLIC FONDUE

SERVES 6

50 g (2 oz) butter or margarine

• • •

1–2 large garlic cloves, chopped finely

• • •

10 green olives, chopped (optional)

• • •

450 ml (¾ pint) double cream

• • •

142 ml (5 fl oz) carton of single cream

• • •

PREPARATION AND COOKING TIME: 10 MINUTES

This fondue makes an unusual and memorable party dish. The flavour of garlic permeates the cream and the aromas which fill the room are quite sensational. The blend of flavours and the creamy texture are irresistible with bread-sticks and crisp crudités.

Melt the butter or margarine in a saucepan over a low heat, add the garlic and olives if used, and simmer for 1–2 minutes. Heat both the creams in a fondue pot, and then add the garlic mixture and stir well.

Simmer the fondue very gently over the fondue burner as you serve it with bread-sticks and a selection of crudités.

GRACE'S SPICY DIP

SERVES 6

500 g (1 lb) fromage frais

• • •

1 tablespoon mango chutney, chopped very finely

• • •

½–1 teaspoon garam masala paste (optional)

• • •

½ teaspoon ground cardamom

• • •

salt to taste

• • •

PREPARATION TIME: 5 MINUTES

The simplest dish in the world to prepare, this recipe was given to me by an American friend of the family called Grace. A creamy dip with a taste of India, the individual spices lift the blandness of the fromage frais. It is lovely served with pitta bread.

Beat the fromage frais with a fork, and fold in all the other ingredients. Beat the mixture until smooth, and check the seasoning. Cover with clingfilm and chill until ready for use.

SKORDALIA

SERVES 6

4 thick slices of white bread

• • •

4 garlic cloves, crushed

• • •

5–6 tablespoons olive oil

• • •

1–2 tablespoons water

• • •

1 tablespoon lemon juice

• • •

salt to taste

• • •

PREPARATION TIME: 15 MINUTES

This is a favourite dish of mine from Greece. It is so simple, yet absolutely delicious as a starter or to go with drinks before a meal. Serve it with crudités such as carrots, cucumber, green pepper, cauliflower, courgettes and celery.

Remove the crusts and process the bread to crumbs. Mix the crumbs with the garlic and stir in the oil gradually, as for mayonnaise (page 158), mixing it slowly until the oil is absorbed. Add a little water at the end of the process and then stir in the lemon juice. The mixture should be fairly thin. Season to taste with salt and serve.

CHAPTER TWO

EGGS AND
CHEESE

WATERCRESS AND GRUYÈRE SOUFFLÉ

SERVES 4

40 g (1½ oz) butter or margarine, plus extra for greasing

• • •

a bunch of watercress, chopped very finely

• • •

2 tablespoons plain flour

• • •

150 ml (¼ pint) milk, warmed

• • •

50 g (2 oz) Gruyère or medium-hard cheese of your choice, grated

• • •

4 eggs, separated

• • •

salt and pepper to taste

• • •

PREPARATION TIME: 35 MINUTES + 20–25 MINUTES COOKING

The two strong and distinctive tastes in this recipe complement each other perfectly and make a really excellent soufflé. I like to serve it with small new potatoes and a simple tossed green salad of frisée and cos lettuce.

Heat 15 g (½ oz) of the butter or margarine in a small saucepan, add the watercress, and cook gently for 2–3 minutes, or until it softens. Set it to one side. Melt the remaining butter or margarine in a saucepan, add the flour, and stir until it is absorbed by the fat. Add the milk a little at a time, stirring constantly so that the mixture is smooth. Cook gently over a low heat for 5 minutes, stirring all the time. Then stir in the cheese, mixing it in well until it has melted. Add the watercress, stir the mixture thoroughly and remove it from the heat. Season to taste with salt and pepper.

Preheat the oven to Gas Mark 6/200°C/400°F. Beat the egg yolks thoroughly and stir into the mixture. Then beat the egg whites until they are very stiff, and fold them in quickly. Grease a 22 cm (8½-inch) soufflé dish and pour in the mixture. Bake for 20–25 minutes until the soufflé is well risen and golden on top, but still slightly moist and runny in the centre. Serve immediately.

PICTURED ON PAGE 10

ARTICHOKE SOUFFLÉ-OMELETTE

SERVES 4

375 g (12 oz) jerusalem artichokes, peeled
· · ·
75 g (3 oz) Gruyère or medium-hard cheese of your choice, grated
· · ·
5 tablespoons Béchamel Sauce (page 158) or soured cream
· · ·
4 eggs, separated
· · ·
1 garlic clove, crushed (optional)
· · ·
salt and pepper to taste
· · ·
oil for frying
· · ·
chopped parsley, to garnish
· · ·
PREPARATION TIME: 25 MINUTES + 15 MINUTES COOKING

The soufflé-omelette is a wonderful invention – it is quicker and easier than a soufflé and more impressive than an omelette. It looks as if you've been creating masterpieces in the kitchen for hours! But this amazing dish is made in a matter of minutes, and it makes a wonderful main course served with french fries and mange tout.

Cook the artichokes in boiling water for about 10 minutes, until they are tender but not too soft. Allow them to cool a little and then cut them into small cubes. Stir the artichokes and cheese into the béchamel sauce or soured cream until they are all well mixed. Beat the egg yolks and stir them into the mixture, and add the garlic if used. Season to taste with salt and pepper. Beat the egg whites very stiffly and fold them into the artichoke mixture.

Grease a large, heavy frying-pan (or two small ones) with a liberal coating of oil, and heat it through. Pour in the mixture and cook over a gentle heat for about 10 minutes, being careful that the bottom does not burn, until the soufflé-omelette begins to puff and set. Then place it under a medium-hot grill for about 3 minutes until the top is set and cooked through, and begins to turn golden. Serve immediately, sprinkled with chopped parsley.

TIROPITTA

SERVES 8

4 eggs
· · ·
375 g (12 oz) feta cheese
· · ·
250 g (8 oz) cottage cheese
· · ·
50 g (2 oz) vegetarian Cheddar cheese, grated
· · ·
2 tablespoons finely chopped parsley, or 1 tablespoon dried mixed herbs
· · ·
75 g (3 oz) butter or margarine, melted
· · ·
375 g (12 oz) fillo pastry
· · ·
pepper and ½ teaspoon grated nutmeg to taste
· · ·
PREPARATION TIME: 25 MINUTES + 40 MINUTES COOKING

A dish from Greece, this is a succulent cheese pie. Soft cheeses – feta and cottage cheese – nestle in a case of crispy fillo pastry. Wonderful with small new potatoes and a tossed salad of watercress, Little Gem lettuce and sliced baby courgettes.

Beat the eggs lightly with a fork, and season to taste with pepper and nutmeg. Drain the feta and crumble it into the eggs using a fork. Add the cottage cheese and the Cheddar, mix them in well, and then stir in the herbs.

Preheat the oven to Gas Mark 5/190°C/375°F. Grease a 20 cm (8-inch) square baking tin with a little of the melted butter or margarine. Spread 7 or 8 layers of fillo pastry over the base and up the sides of the tin, brushing each layer with melted butter or margarine. Cover the fillo evenly with the cheese mixture, then top with 5 or 6 more layers of fillo, brushing them with melted fat as before. Turn in the edges. Give the top layer of fillo a generous brushing with melted fat so that it will turn a deep golden colour.

Bake the pie for 40 minutes, or until deeply browned. If you are making it in advance, cook it for 25 minutes only; then return it to the oven for a further 15 minutes before it is served. Allow it to stand for 5 minutes; then cut it into 8 with a sharp knife, and lift it out of the tin.

*Cauliflower and lovage soufflé
Artichoke soufflé-omelette
Mozzarella in carrozza
Oeufs Dijonnaise
Devilled eggs with chilli*

OEUFS POCHÉS SUR CHAMPIGNONS

SERVES 4

4 large flat mushrooms

· · ·

25 g (1 oz) butter or margarine

· · ·

4 eggs

· · ·

salt and pepper to taste

· · ·

4 tablespoons Garlic Sesame Croûtons (page 19)

· · ·

PREPARATION AND COOKING TIME: 10–15 MINUTES

A luscious meal of softly cooked eggs on tasty flat mushrooms, and sprinkled with croûtons. Lovely for breakfast, or at suppertime.

Remove the stalks from the mushrooms and reserve them for another use, and then wipe the caps clean. Steam them over boiling water for about 10 minutes, or until soft. Alternatively, place them in a large flat dish and microwave them for 3 minutes, and then leave them to stand while you cook the eggs.

Heat a large, heavy frying-pan. Melt the butter or margarine so it covers the base of the pan evenly. Over a moderate heat, break the eggs carefully into the pan and cook them gently until the white sets and the yolk is still runny.

Place one mushroom cap on each serving plate and season to taste with salt and pepper. Carefully place one cooked egg inside each cap, and sprinkle with the croûtons. Serve immediately.

SOUFFLÉ 'LIGHT FANTASTIC'

SERVES 6

25 g (1 oz) butter or margarine, plus extra for greasing

· · ·

175 g (6 oz) mushrooms, sliced

· · ·

125 g (4 oz) sorrel or lettuce leaves, shredded

· · ·

300 g (10 oz) small courgettes, sliced

· · ·

150 ml (¼ pint) Béchamel Sauce (page 158)

· · ·

40 g (1½ oz) hard cheese, grated

· · ·

2 eggs, plus 2 extra egg whites

· · ·

salt and pepper to taste

· · ·

PREPARATION TIME: 30 MINUTES + 30–35 MINUTES COOKING

This soufflé is a party piece, spectacular both to look at and to taste. It takes some time to prepare, but it is certainly worth the effort – the courgette purée makes a fabulous base for the main soufflé, and then in the middle lies a layer of mushrooms and sorrel.

To make the filling, heat the butter or margarine in a saucepan, add the mushrooms, and sauté quickly until they are cooked through but still crisp. Remove them with a slotted spoon and add the sorrel or lettuce to the pan. Lower the heat and cook for about 5 minutes, stirring all the time. Stir the sorrel or lettuce into the mushrooms and season to taste with salt and pepper. Set aside.

Steam the courgettes over boiling water until tender (about 5–7 minutes); then purée them with the béchamel sauce. Stir in the cheese and mix thoroughly; then stir in the well-beaten egg yolks. Season to taste with salt and pepper.

Preheat the oven to Gas Mark 5/190°C/375°F. Beat all four egg whites until they are very stiff and fold them into the soufflé mixture. Put half the mixture into a well-greased 20 cm (8-inch) soufflé dish, and cover it with the mushroom filling. Spread the remaining soufflé mixture on top, and bake for 25–35 minutes or until the soufflé is risen and set but still moist and slightly runny in the middle.

CUCUMBER AND CHEESE MOUSSE

SERVES 6–8

1 large cucumber, peeled and diced finely

. . .

125 g (4 oz) curd cheese

. . .

50 g (2 oz) vegetarian Cheddar cheese, grated finely

. . .

250 g (8 oz) greek-style yogurt

. . .

1 tablespoon grated onion

. . .

2 tablespoons white wine vinegar

. . .

1 tablespoon caster sugar

. . .

1 teaspoon ground coriander

. . .

15 g (½ oz) agar-agar

. . .

150 ml (¼ pint) vegetable stock

. . .

sunflower oil for greasing

. . .

salt and pepper to taste

. . .

a bunch of watercress, trimmed, to garnish

. . .

PREPARATION TIME: 35 MINUTES + 6 HOURS CHILLING

I have used this recipe for years – it is one of my favourites for a summer party or a buffet table. It is light and creamy, and an excellent way of using thick greek yogurt. Its gentle taste is enhanced by a spicy watercress garnish.

Sprinkle the cucumber with salt and place it in a colander, weighted down with a plate, for 30 minutes.

Meanwhile, mash the curd cheese and mix it with the Cheddar cheese, yogurt and onion until thoroughly blended. Stir in the vinegar and sugar and season to taste with pepper and the coriander.

Sprinkle the agar-agar over the stock, bring to the boil and then simmer for 5 minutes or until the agar-agar has dissolved. Stir thoroughly and beat this into the cheese mixture.

Drain the cucumber thoroughly and fold it into the cheese mixture. Pour into a well-oiled 1.2 litre (2-pint) ring-mould to set. Chill for at least 6 hours, or overnight.

When ready to serve, turn the mousse out on to a platter and garnish with watercress in the centre of the ring.

PICTURED ON TITLE PAGE

CAULIFLOWER AND LOVAGE SOUFFLÉ

SERVES 4

1 medium-size cauliflower, separated into florets

. . .

150 ml (¼ pint) Béchamel Sauce (page 158)

. . .

25 g (1 oz) hard cheese, grated

. . .

a medium bunch of lovage, chopped finely, or 50–75 g (2–3 oz) celery leaves, chopped finely

. . .

3 eggs, separated

. . .

2 tablespoons double cream

. . .

butter or margarine for greasing

. . .

salt and pepper to taste

. . .

PREPARATION TIME: 30 MINUTES + 20–25 MINUTES COOKING

This simple combination of two delicate ingredients makes a light and quite distinctive soufflé, once fresh lovage is available. Serve it with a tomato and onion salad and fresh Granary bread, for a light but delectable lunch, alfresco if the weather permits.

Steam the cauliflower over boiling water for about 15 minutes, or until tender. Liquidise it to a rough purée with the béchamel sauce and season to taste with salt and pepper. Stir in the cheese and lovage or celery leaves and mix well.

Preheat the oven to Gas Mark 6/200°C/400°F. Beat the egg yolks thoroughly and fold them into the soufflé mixture, and then stir in the cream. Beat the egg whites until they are very stiff, and fold them quickly into the mixture. Pour the soufflé mixture into a well-greased 15–18 cm (6–7-inch) soufflé dish and bake for 20–25 minutes until well risen and set, but still slightly runny in the middle. Serve immediately.

MOZZARELLA IN CARROZZA

SERVES 4

8 thin slices of day-old bread, crusts removed

. . .

125 g (4 oz) mozzarella cheese, sliced

. . .

2 eggs, beaten

. . .

oil for deep-frying

PREPARATION AND COOKING TIME: 15 MINUTES

I have adapted this traditional Italian idea in a recipe that is easy to prepare and simple to cook. They are popular morsels which make a light, nutritious and tempting meal served with a tossed salad using a variety of lettuces of different colours and textures.

Make sandwiches with the bread and mozzarella and cut them into 5 cm (2-inch) squares. Press them down well and soak them in the beaten egg for about 2–3 minutes on each side. Heat the oil to 190°C/375°F, add the sandwiches and deep-fry them until they are golden and crisp all over. Drain them on kitchen paper and serve as soon as possible.

GOLDEN CHEESE WON-TONS

SERVES 4

100 g (3½ oz) round goat cheese

. . .

150 g (5 oz) won-ton skins (sixteen 8 cm/3-inch skins)

. . .

groundnut oil for deep-frying

. . .

PREPARATION TIME: 5 MINUTES + 5–10 MINUTES COOKING

These are delicious served with a mixed salad of lollo rosso, radicchio and sliced radishes, tossed in Garlic Vinaigrette (page 133).

Cut the cheese into thin rounds. Place each round of cheese in the centre of a won-ton skin, moisten the edges, and place another won-ton skin on top. Pinch the edges together between your fingertips. Heat the oil to 190°C/375°F and deep-fry the won-tons until they are puffed and golden-brown. Drain them on kitchen paper and serve as soon as possible.

TARTE AU FROMAGE

SERVES 4

FOR THE PASTRY

. . .

175 g (6 oz) plain flour

. . .

½ teaspoon salt

. . .

75 g (3 oz) butter or margarine, plus extra for greasing

. . .

2–4 tablespoons cold water

FOR THE FILLING

. . .

25 g (1 oz) butter or margarine

. . .

2 tablespoons plain flour

. . .

150 ml (¼ pint) warm milk

. . .

a pinch of nutmeg

. . .

50 g (2 oz) Gruyère or medium-hard cheese of your choice, grated

. . .

25 g (1 oz) hard cheese, grated

. . .

2 eggs, separated

. . .

pepper and chilli powder (Cayenne) to taste

. . .

PREPARATION TIME: 25 MINUTES + 1 HOUR CHILLING + 25–30 MINUTES COOKING

I have been making this tart for years, and it never fails to work, nor to delight. It is light, like a soufflé in a pastry shell, and is best eaten straight from the oven.

Preheat the oven to Gas Mark 6/200°C/400°F. Sift the flour with the salt and rub in the butter or margarine until the mixture resembles breadcrumbs. Add the water and form the pastry into a ball. Roll lightly and use to line a greased 20 cm (8-inch) flan tin. Chill for 30 minutes. Prick the surface evenly with a fork, cover with foil or greaseproof paper weighted with dried beans, and bake blind for 10–15 minutes.

Meanwhile, melt the butter or margarine in a saucepan and stir in the flour. Add the milk a little at a time, stirring constantly until the sauce is smooth. Season with the nutmeg, and pepper and a little chilli powder to taste. Cook gently over a very low heat for 5–6 minutes, stirring occasionally.

Remove the pan from the heat and stir in the grated cheeses until they have melted, and then stir in the well-beaten egg yolks. Whisk the egg whites until very stiff, and fold them quickly in. Pour the mixture into the pastry shell and return it to the oven for 12–15 minutes, or until the filling is risen and golden-brown, but still a little creamy inside.

SAVOURY CHEESE AND VEGETABLE CLAFOUTIS

SERVES 4–6

3 eggs

• • •

175 g (6 oz) plain flour

• • •

450 ml (³⁄₄ pint) milk

• • •

a pinch of salt

• • •

500 g (1 lb) courgettes

• • •

175 g (6 oz) vegetarian Cheddar cheese, grated

• • •

1 teaspoon dried mixed herbs

• • •

425 g (14 oz) broccoli and cauliflower florets

• • •

125 g (4 oz) mange tout, trimmed

• • •

25 g (1 oz) butter or margarine

• • •

4 tablespoons olive oil

PREPARATION TIME: 30 MINUTES + 45–50 MINUTES COOKING

A vegetarian version of toad in the hole! This is based on a classic French recipe that is usually associated with desserts: I tried it out as a savoury course, and it is a revelation. Serve it with warm french bread or Thyme Oatcakes (page 124) and a salad of your choice (pages 125–138).

Whisk the eggs and fold in the flour slowly, beating until the mixture is smooth. Add the milk a little at a time, beating constantly until you have a smooth batter. Add the salt.

Grate half the courgettes and fold these into the batter with the cheese and herbs. Slice the remaining courgettes very thinly. Cut the broccoli and cauliflower into tiny florets and slice them thinly. Slice the mange tout into diagonal strips.

Preheat the oven to Gas Mark 5/190°C/375°F. Heat the butter or margarine in a saucepan with the olive oil, add the sliced vegetables and gently fry for about 5 minutes, or until they are soft. Place the sautéed vegetables in the base of an ovenproof baking dish, and pour the batter over them. Bake for 40–50 minutes, or until well risen and golden-brown, and a sharp knife inserted into the centre comes out clean.

PICTURED ON TITLE PAGE

MELTING CAMEMBERT COOKIES

MAKES 10

175 g (6 oz) ripe Camembert or vegetarian Brie

• • •

15 g (¹⁄₂ oz) butter or margarine, softened, plus extra for greasing

• • •

¹⁄₂ teaspoon ground cumin

• • •

1 egg yolk

• • •

flour for rolling

• • •

1 whole egg, beaten

• • •

PREPARATION TIME: 15 MINUTES + 15 MINUTES COOKING

These succulent golden circles of melted cheese coated in a crust of lightly beaten egg are irresistible. As they cook they spread out into circles like cookies, and are just as delicious. They make a wonderful starter served with a helping of shredded crisp lettuce dressed in Garlic Vinaigrette (page 133), or with the Japanese Five-colour Salad (page 125).

Preheat the oven to Gas Mark 6/200°C/400°F. Remove the rind from the Camembert and grate the cheese coarsely – this will reduce it to a mush. Mash it with the butter or margarine, season with the cumin, and then beat in the egg yolk. Divide the mixture into dessertspoon-size portions and form into small ball-shapes. Roll each cookie in a little flour, and then dip it into the beaten egg. Place the cookies on a large greased baking sheet, set well apart. Bake for 15 minutes, and serve immediately.

PICTURED ON PAGE 135

FOLLOWING PAGE (CLOCKWISE)
Tiropitta
Tarte au fromage
Soufflé 'light fantastic'
Cheese ring with summer herbs and red sauce
Parsley and garlic eggs
Oeufs pochés sur champignons
Escargot butter (PAGE 153)
Golden cheese won-tons

PARSLEY AND GARLIC EGGS

SERVES 2

40 g (1 1/2 oz) butter or margarine

· · ·

2 tablespoons finely chopped parsley

· · ·

1 large garlic clove, crushed

· · ·

4 tablespoons double cream

· · ·

4 eggs

· · ·

15 g (1/2 oz) parmesan or vegetarian Cheddar cheese, grated

· · ·

salt and pepper to taste

· · ·

PREPARATION TIME: 10 MINUTES

Parsley is reputed to extinguish the smell of garlic on the breath, and so I use lots of it: not only as an excuse for eating as much garlic as possible, but also because it is such a delicious herb. This scrumptious combination of a creamy garlic butter with eggs makes a rich but wonderful quick first course or lunch dish.

Melt the butter in a heavy frying-pan over a very gentle heat, and stir in the parsley, garlic and cream. Mix well and then break the eggs into the frying-pan and cook very gently until lightly set. Season to taste with salt and pepper, sprinkle with the cheese and serve immediately, with all the juices from the pan poured over the top.

DEVILLED EGGS WITH CHILLI

SERVES 4

230 g (7 oz) can of tomatoes

· · ·

1 teaspoon dried mixed herbs

· · ·

1 tablespoon Worcestershire sauce

· · ·

1/2–1 teaspoon chilli powder (Cayenne)

· · ·

1 shallot or onion, chopped

· · ·

150 ml (1/4 pint) white wine

· · ·

8 eggs

· · ·

olive oil for frying

· · ·

salt and pepper to taste

· · ·

PREPARATION AND COOKING TIME: 25 MINUTES

This is brilliant for a quick meal. The sauce, spiced with hot chilli powder (Cayenne), is poured over sizzling eggs, and you need no more than wholemeal rolls and a side salad to make a quick, light meal.

Place the tomatoes, herbs, Worcestershire sauce, and chilli powder in a saucepan and season to taste with salt and pepper. Simmer gently, stirring constantly to break up the tomatoes. Meanwhile, simmer the shallot or onion in the wine for 4–5 minutes or until the wine is reduced by half. Stir it into the tomato sauce and keep warm over a very low heat.

Heat the oil in a frying-pan, add the eggs and fry them for a minute or so until they are sizzling and set. Serve two eggs per person with the sauce spooned over them.

CHEESE RING WITH SUMMER HERBS AND RED SAUCE

SERVES 4–6

FOR THE CHEESE RING

• • •

50 g (2 oz) butter or margarine, plus extra for greasing

• • •

300 ml (½ pint) milk

• • •

25 g (1 oz) fresh white breadcrumbs

• • •

250 g (8 oz) vegetarian Cheddar cheese, grated

• • •

250 g (8 oz) cooked long-grain rice

• • •

2 tablespoons chopped onion

• • •

6 tablespoons finely chopped herbs, such as sage, chives, thyme or marjoram, or 2 tablespoons mixed dried herbs

• • •

2 eggs, beaten thoroughly

• • •

salt and pepper to taste

• • •

FOR THE RED SAUCE

• • •

150 ml (¼ pint) Mayonnaise (page 158)

• • •

4 tablespoons tomato purée

• • •

2 tablespoons chopped basil

• • •

a pinch of paprika

• • •

a pinch of sugar

• • •

salt to taste

• • •

sprigs of the herbs in flower (optional), to garnish

PREPARATION TIME: 40 MINUTES + 35–40 MINUTES BAKING + 2 HOURS CHILLING

This is one of my faithful stand-bys for summer buffets. It looks so colourful with the red sauce poured into the centre, and it has a creamy, melt-in-the-mouth texture. A marvellous centrepiece when surrounded by a range of salads (pages 125–138).

Preheat the oven to Gas Mark 4/180°C/350°F. Melt the butter or margarine in a large saucepan and heat it with the milk. Add the breadcrumbs and cheese and stir over a low heat until the cheese has melted and the sauce is smooth. Mix in the rice and onion, stirring constantly over a gentle heat until everything is thoroughly mixed. Season to taste with salt and pepper and stir in the herbs. Finally, mix in the beaten eggs and then pour the mixture into a well-greased 900 ml (1½ pint) ring-mould. Set this in a roasting tin of hot water about 2.5–5 cm (1–2 inches) deep, and bake for 35–40 minutes, or until set and browned. Cool, and loosen the edges of the cheese ring with a knife; then put a flat serving dish on top, invert, and lift off the ring-mould.

To make the sauce, mix the mayonnaise with the tomato purée and basil. Season to taste with the paprika, sugar, and salt. Fill the centre of the ring with this sauce and chill for 2 hours.

Garnish the cheese ring with sprigs and flowers of the herbs you have used, if you like.

OEUFS DIJONNAISE

SERVES 4 OR 8

8 eggs

• • •

300 ml (½ pint) Béchamel Sauce (page 158)

• • •

2 tablespoons Dijon mustard

• • •

50 g (2 oz) Gruyère or medium-hard cheese of your choice, grated

• • •

5 tablespoons single cream

• • •

salt and pepper to taste

• • •

parsley sprigs, to garnish

PREPARATION AND COOKING TIME: 30 MINUTES

The sauce for this dish is inspired by the famous mustard of Dijon: it is enriched with cream and a medium-hard cheese such as Gruyère and is a delicious way of transforming soft-boiled eggs into an elegant dish. You can also serve it as an appetising starter, serving one egg per person on a bed of crispy lettuce.

Put the eggs into boiling water for exactly 4 minutes; then plunge them under cold running water until they are completely cold. Meanwhile, warm the béchamel sauce; check and adjust the seasoning. Stir in the mustard and cheese and stir the sauce over a low heat until it is well blended. Thin it out with the cream, heat it through and check the seasoning again. Peel the eggs very carefully. Place two on each plate and spoon the sauce over them. Garnish with the parsley sprigs and serve at once.

CHAPTER THREE

PANCAKES, FRITTERS AND BEIGNETS

FRITTER BATTER

MAKES 300 ML (½ PINT)

125 g (4 oz) plain flour
· · ·
a pinch of salt
· · ·
3 tablespoons vegetable oil
· · ·
150 ml (¼ pint) warm water
· · ·
1 egg white
· · ·

PREPARATION TIME: 10 MINUTES + 2 HOURS STANDING

Sift the flour with the salt and stir in the oil. Gradually add the water, stirring well until the mixture is thick and creamy. Allow it to stand in a cool place for 2 hours and then add about 2 tablespoons cold water to thin it out.

Beat the egg white until it is very stiff, and then fold it into the batter just before you are ready to use it.

To deep-fry fritters, use a deep-frying pan with a basket that will lift the fritters out and drain them at the same time. Use light, clean vegetable oil – preferably groundnut oil which is tasteless – to about two-thirds of the way up the pan. Heat the oil to 190°C/375°F, using a thermometer to gauge the temperature. Lower the heat to moderate once the required temperature has been reached, and during the deep-frying. Add the fritters and deep-fry them, turning them so that they are golden all over.

Shake the fritters in the basket over the pan, and then drain them thoroughly on kitchen paper. All deep-fried food is best eaten as soon as possible, with the batter thoroughly drained and crisp.

Buckwheat blinis
Stir-fried leek and mushroom pancakes
Potato and courgette fritters
Cauliflower fritters with Stilton sauce

SPICY MUSHROOM PAKORAS

SERVES 4

FOR THE PAKORAS
• • •
1 quantity Fritter Batter (page 40)
• • •
1 teaspoon ground cumin
• • •
1 teaspoon ground coriander
• • •
1 teaspoon ground turmeric
• • •
250 g (8 oz) button mushrooms
• • •
vegetable oil for frying
• • •
FOR THE DIPPING SAUCE
• • •
5 tablespoons soy sauce
• • •
1 tablespoon white wine vinegar
• • •
2.5 cm (1-inch) piece of root ginger, peeled and grated finely
• • •
a dash of Tabasco sauce
• • •

PREPARATION TIME: 15 MINUTES + 2 HOURS STANDING + 10–15 MINUTES COOKING

I had the most wonderful mushroom pakoras on a trip to India some time ago. Sitting in a garden under a cascade of scarlet blossom, beneath a scorching blue sky, I ate these morsels coated in spicy batter. They always remind me of that hot day in Jaipur, and the intense Indian heat.

Mix the spices into the batter before leaving it to stand for 2 hours.

To make the dipping sauce, mix together all the ingredients and leave to stand while you make the pakoras.

Cut the mushrooms in half and dip them into the prepared batter. Heat the oil to 190°C/375°F in a large deep-frying pan, add the pakoras in 4 batches and deep-fry each batch for 2–3 minutes, turning the mushrooms so that they are golden all over (page 40). Drain on kitchen paper and keep them warm in the oven until they are all cooked. Serve as soon as possible with the dipping sauce.

CAULIFLOWER FRITTERS WITH STILTON SAUCE

SERVES 4

1 medium-size cauliflower, separated into florets
• • •
150 ml (¼ pint) Béchamel Sauce (page 158)
• • •
50 g (2 oz) Stilton or Danish blue cheese, mashed
• • •
125 ml (4 fl oz) crème fraîche or soured cream
• • •
1 quantity Fritter Batter (page 40)
• • •
vegetable oil for frying
• • •

PREPARATION TIME: 10 MINUTES + 10 MINUTES COOKING

These light, mouth-watering morsels make a delightful starter to a meal. The thin, delicate cheese sauce and cauliflower are irresistible served with Nasturtium Harlequin Salad (page 138).

Steam the cauliflower florets lightly over boiling water for about 4–5 minutes so that they are still crisp and then allow them to cool. Smoothly blend the béchamel sauce with the cheese. Add the cream and blend again. Heat the sauce gently.

Heat the oil to 190°C/375°F in a large deep-frying pan, dip the cauliflower florets in the batter and add them to the pan. Deep-fry the fritters for 3–4 minutes, turning them until they are golden all over (page 40). Drain on kitchen paper and serve as soon as possible with the sauce.

ONION BHAJIA

> **SERVES 4**

1 quantity Fritter Batter (page 40)
. . .
1 teaspoon ground cumin
. . .
1 teaspoon ground coriander
. . .
1 teaspoon ground turmeric
. . .
vegetable oil for deep-frying
. . .
2 medium-size onions, sliced thinly
. . .
FOR THE CUCUMBER RAITA
. . .
½ cucumber, peeled and grated
. . .
150 ml (¼ pint) natural yogurt
. . .
½ teaspoon ground cumin
. . .
a sprinkling of paprika, to garnish
. . .
PREPARATION TIME: 20 MINUTES + 15–20 MINUTES COOKING

These crispy onion rings use the same spiced batter as Spicy Mushroom Pakoras (opposite) and are served with a cooling raita. I like to serve them with drinks before a light meal, and they are one of the most popular snacks among my family and friends.

Mix the spices into the batter before leaving it to stand for 2 hours.

To make the raita, combine the cucumber with the yogurt and cumin. Sprinkle with a little paprika and chill the raita while you make the bhajia.

Heat the oil to 190°C/375°F in a large deep-frying pan, dip the onion rings in 4 batches in the prepared batter so they are well coated and deep-fry each batch for about 4–5 minutes until the bhajia are very crisp and golden all over (page 40). Drain on kitchen paper and serve as soon as possible with the raita.

POTATO AND COURGETTE FRITTERS

> **SERVES 4–6**

375 g (12 oz) potatoes, peeled
. . .
375 g (12 oz) courgettes
. . .
2 eggs, beaten lightly
. . .
2 tablespoons olive oil
. . .
25 g (1 oz) butter or margarine
. . .
salt, pepper and grated nutmeg to taste
. . .
PREPARATION TIME: 25 MINUTES + 15–20 MINUTES COOKING

These make a different kind of fritter from the ones that are dipped in batter; with these, a mixture of grated potato and courgette is mixed with egg and shallow-fried in oil. They are delicious with a crisp salad for a simple meal, or as a side vegetable.

Grate the courgettes and potatoes coarsely. Put them in a sieve and press down with the back of a wooden spoon to extract much of their moisture, and then pat them dry on kitchen paper. Add the beaten eggs and season to taste with salt, pepper and nutmeg. Mix well.

Heat the oil with the butter or margarine in a heavy frying-pan and fry the mixture in tablespoonfuls, pressing each fritter down with a fork. Cook the fritters gently for about 3 minutes, turning them so that they are browned on both sides. Drain them on kitchen paper and keep them warm. Continue in this way, stirring the mixture before each batch of fritters is added to the pan and replenishing the oil and butter or margarine mixture in the pan as necessary, until all the potato and courgette mixture has been used.

OKRA BEIGNETS

SERVES 4

50 g (2 oz) butter or margarine

• • •

about 5 tablespoons cold water

• • •

50 g (2 oz) plain flour, sifted

• • •

a pinch of salt

• • •

3 eggs, beaten well

• • •

vegetable oil for deep-frying

• • •

375 g (12 oz) small okra

• • •

2 tablespoons sesame oil

• • •

2.5 cm (1-inch) piece of root ginger, peeled and grated finely

• • •

1 large garlic clove, crushed

• • •

3 tablespoons soy sauce

• • •

PREPARATION AND COOKING TIME: 10–15 MINUTES

Although you need to go to a certain amount of trouble to prepare these, they are worth every minute spent on them! The soft texture of the okra is scrumptious inside their crisp choux-beignet cases, and the touch of ginger and garlic is sensational. You can adapt this recipe for other vegetables, too: courgettes and cauliflower are both particularly good.

To make the choux paste, melt the butter or margarine in a saucepan with the water. Stir in the flour and salt and mix well until thoroughly blended and smooth. Remove the pan from the heat, cool slightly and beat in the eggs gradually until the mixture is glossy. Heat the oil to 190°C/375°F in a large deep-frying pan, add the mixture a tablespoonful at a time and deep-fry for 1–2 minutes until the beignets puff up (page 40). Turn them until they are golden all over. Drain on kitchen paper.

Steam the okra over boiling water for about 6–8 minutes, or until tender. Heat the oil, stir in the ginger and garlic, and cook gently for 3–4 minutes. Then add the soy sauce, heat it gently and toss in the okra. Cook until the okra are well coated, and then place them inside the golden choux puffs. Serve immediately.

BASIC PANCAKE BATTER

MAKES 12

150 g (5 oz) plain flour, sifted

• • •

a pinch of salt

• • •

2 eggs

• • •

300 ml (½ pint) milk

• • •

150 ml (¼ pint) water

• • •

2 teaspoons vegetable oil, plus extra for frying

PREPARATION TIME: 5 MINUTES + 3 HOURS STANDING + 30 MINUTES COOKING

Blend together all the ingredients smoothly and allow the mixture to stand for about 3 hours before using.

Stir the mixture thoroughly, and thin it with a little water if necessary. Heat the oil in a large frying-pan, and pour in sufficient pancake batter to cover the base. Cook the pancake for about 30 seconds or until it is golden brown underneath, then flip it over and cook the other side. Remove and keep warm until all the pancake batter has been used.

GÂTEAU DE CRÊPES

> SERVES 6–8

1 quantity Basic Pancake Batter, made into 12 pancakes (opposite)

FOR THE FILLINGS
· · ·
600 ml (1 pint) Béchamel Sauce (page 158)
· · ·
175 g (6 oz) vegetarian Cheddar cheese, grated
· · ·
5 tablespoons single cream
· · ·
FOR THE CHEESE AND MUSHROOM LAYER
· · ·
250 g (8 oz) cottage cheese
· · ·
1 egg, beaten
· · ·
15 g (½ oz) butter or margarine
· · ·
125 g (4oz) mushrooms, sliced
· · ·
1 tablespoon chopped spring onions
· · ·
salt and pepper to taste
· · ·
FOR THE SPINACH LAYER
· · ·
375 g (12 oz) spinach
· · ·
FOR THE ASPARAGUS AND TOMATO LAYER
· · ·
375 g (12 oz) asparagus
· · ·
397 g (14 oz) can of chopped tomatoes, drained
· · ·
FOR THE TOPPING
· · ·
25 g (1 oz) hard cheese, grated finely
· · ·
15 g (½ oz) butter or margarine, plus extra for greasing

PREPARATION TIME: 40 MINUTES + 25–30 MINUTES COOKING

A party piece, made from layers of pancakes filled with alternating fillings of cheese and mushroom, creamed spinach, and asparagus and tomato. The gâteau is cut into wedges, and both looks and tastes sensational. Serve with a salad of chinese leaves and iceberg lettuce.

Warm the béchamel sauce over a gentle heat. Add the cheese and stir until it melts. Stir in the cream and heat again.

Mash the cottage cheese and mix it with the beaten egg. Season to taste with salt and pepper, and then add 150 ml (¼ pint) of the cheese sauce. Melt the butter or margarine in a saucepan, add the mushrooms and spring onions, and sauté for about 5 minutes, or until they are soft. Then add these to the cheese mixture, stirring well. Check the seasoning.

Lightly cook the spinach in boiling water for about 5 minutes; drain and then squeeze out any excess water. Chop it and mix with 150 ml (¼ pint) of the cheese sauce. Check the seasoning.

Lightly cook the asparagus in boiling water for about 10–15 minutes. Cut into 2.5 cm (1-inch) lengths. Mix the vegetables with a further 150 ml (¼ pint) of the cheese sauce.

Preheat the oven to Gas Mark 4/180°C/350°F. Grease a 25 cm (10-inch) ovenproof dish and stack in it layers of pancakes, spreading them with alternate fillings. Finish with the remaining cheese sauce and sprinkle the top with grated cheese, dotted with the butter or margarine. Bake for 25–30 minutes. Allow to stand for 5 minutes before cutting.

PICTURED ON PAGE 11

MUSHROOM BUTTERFLIES

> MAKES 18

12 sheets of fillo pastry
· · ·
50 g (2 oz) butter or margarine, melted
· · ·
18 small button mushrooms
· · ·
vegetable oil for deep-frying

PREPARATION AND COOKING TIME: 10–15 MINUTES

Little twists of fillo have a single mushroom as their filling, which keeps all its flavour sealed as it cooks in the deep, hot oil. These golden morsels are best eaten straight from the pan, as a snack or a starter.

Take 4 sheets of the fillo at a time, and brush them with the melted butter or margarine, keeping the remaining sheets covered with a damp tea towel or clingfilm to prevent drying and cracking. Place the 4 sheets on top of each other, and cut into six 13 × 13 cm (5 × 5-inch) squares. Place one mushroom in the centre of each square, and roll it up. Twist the ends around like a sweet-wrapper and fan them out. Repeat twice more to make 18 pastry twists in total.

Heat the oil to 190°C/375°F in a large deep-frying pan, press down the fillo pastry twists and deep-fry them for 3–4 minutes, turning them until they are golden on both sides (page 40). Drain on kitchen paper and keep warm until ready to serve. Eat as soon as possible.

PICTURED ON TITLE PAGE

SPICY VEGETABLE CRÊPES

SERVES 4–6

1 quantity Basic Pancake Batter (page 44)

· · ·

2 teaspoons ground turmeric

· · ·

FOR THE FILLING

· · ·

175 g (6 oz) green lentils, soaked for 1 hour

· · ·

1 onion, chopped

· · ·

1 bay leaf

· · ·

2.5 cm (1-inch) piece of root ginger, peeled and bruised

· · ·

1 whole chilli (optional)

· · ·

2 teaspoons ground cumin

· · ·

2 teaspoons ground coriander

· · ·

3 tablespoons sesame oil

· · ·

1 small crisp lettuce, shredded

· · ·

125 g (4 oz) each cooked broccoli, peas and courgettes or mushrooms

· · ·

25 g (1 oz) hard cheese, grated finely

· · ·

butter or margarine for greasing

· · ·

salt to taste

· · ·

PREPARATION TIME: 50–60 MINUTES + 1 HOUR SOAKING
+ 3½ HOURS STANDING + 15 MINUTES COOKING

A warmly satisfying mixture of lentils and chopped vegetables, lightly spiced with cumin and coriander, ginger and a touch of chilli, makes a meal of these stuffed pancakes. The addition of lightly cooked, shredded lettuce is an original touch for a perfect supper dish.

Mix the turmeric into the pancake batter before allowing it to stand, as instructed (page 44), before using to make 12 pancakes.

Drain the soaked lentils and put them into a saucepan with water to just cover. Bring to the boil with the onion, bay leaf,

ginger and chilli if used, and then cover and simmer for 25–30 minutes or until the lentils are soft. Drain off any excess water, remove the bay leaf, ginger and chilli, and stir in the spices. Leave the mixture to stand, covered, for 30 minutes, and then season to taste with salt.

Meanwhile, heat the oil in a saucepan, add the lettuce and cook it gently for about 5 minutes, stirring constantly until it softens. Stir the lettuce into the lentil mixture with the other vegetables.

Preheat the oven to Gas Mark 4/180°C/350°F. Place 3–4 tablespoons of the mixture in the centre of each pancake and roll it up. Grease a large ovenproof dish, place the pancakes in it in a single layer and sprinkle them with the cheese. Bake for 15 minutes.

SMALL POTATO PANCAKES

SERVES 2–3

375 g (12 oz) mashed potatoes

· · ·

1 egg

· · ·

2 tablespoons single cream or milk

· · ·

25 g (1 oz) plain flour

· · ·

50 g (2 oz) butter or margarine, melted

· · ·

salt and pepper to taste

· · ·

PREPARATION TIME: 35 MINUTES + 30 MINUTES STANDING
+ 20–25 MINUTES COOKING

A simple, light batter made with mashed potato and egg is fried in little rounds to make miniature golden pancakes. A side vegetable with a difference.

Blend the potatoes with the egg, cream or milk, flour, and salt and pepper to taste, until smooth. Transfer the batter to a bowl and leave it to stand, covered, for 30 minutes. Heat a heavy frying-pan or griddle over a moderate heat until it is hot, and then brush it with the melted butter or margarine.

Stir the batter. Drop tablespoons of the mixture on to the pan or griddle to form 4–5 cm (1½–2-inch) circles, and cook the pancakes until bubbles appear on the surface. Turn them over and cook on the other side until they are golden. Transfer them to a platter and keep them warm, covered, in a very low oven until ready to serve.

PREVIOUS PAGE (CLOCKWISE)
Small potato pancakes
Spicy potato parcels
Spicy mushroom pakoras
Onion bhajia
Spicy vegetable crêpes
Okra beignets
Vegetable spring rolls

STIR-FRIED LEEK AND MUSHROOM PANCAKES

> SERVES 4–6

1 quantity Basic Pancake Batter (page 44)

• • •

4 tablespoons sesame oil

• • •

3.5 cm (1½-inch) piece of root ginger, peeled and grated

• • •

2 garlic cloves, crushed

• • •

6 spring onions, chopped

• • •

500 g (1 lb) small leeks, chopped finely

• • •

300 g (10 oz) small button mushrooms, quartered

• • •

2 tablespoons soy sauce

• • •

1 teaspoon black bean sauce

• • •

2 tablespoons dry white wine

• • •

PREPARATION TIME: 10 MINUTES + 10 MINUTES COOKING

A deliciously light mixture of leeks and mushrooms simply tossed in oil and lightly seasoned with Chinese spices and sauces. These stuffed crêpes are quick and easy to make, ideal for an informal lunch served perhaps with Salade de Fenouil avec Tomates (page 129) and a watercress salad.

Make the pancakes (page 44) and keep them warm while you make the stuffing.

Heat the oil in a large frying-pan or wok, add the ginger, garlic and spring onions and cook gently for about 4–5 minutes until they are soft. Add the leeks and stir-fry them for about 2–3 minutes until they begin to soften; then add the mushrooms and stir these until well coated in the fat. Add the soy sauce, bean sauce and wine, and carry on stir-frying until the mixture is cooked through but still crisp. Heap 3–4 tablespoons of the mixture into the middle of each pancake, and fold it in half to make a half-moon shape, or in quarters. Serve immediately.

SPICY POTATO PARCELS

> MAKES 6–8

3 medium-size potatoes, cooked and mashed

• • •

1 medium-size onion, chopped

• • •

4 tablespoons chopped parsley

• • •

2 tablespoons chopped coriander

• • •

1 egg

• • •

1 garlic clove, chopped finely

• • •

1 tablespoon olive oil

• • •

1 tablespoon wine vinegar

• • •

1 teaspoon paprika

• • •

1 teaspoon ground cumin

• • •

6–8 large sheets of fillo pastry

butter or margarine for greasing and brushing

salt and pepper to taste

• • •

PREPARATION TIME: 25 MINUTES + 30–40 MINUTES COOKING

These fillo parcels are filled with a spiced mixture of mashed potatoes spiked with green herbs. They are a delightful way to start a meal – or you can serve them as a light lunch dish, with a choice of salads (pages 125–138).

Mix the potatoes with the onion, herbs, egg, garlic, oil and vinegar. Add the spices and season to taste with salt. Mix very thoroughly, using a fork, until well blended.

Preheat the oven to Gas Mark 6/200°C/400°F. Cut a sheet of fillo pastry in half, widthways, keeping the remaining sheets covered with a damp tea towel to prevent drying and cracking. Brush each surface with oil and place one half on top of the other. Place 2 tablespoons of the mixture in the middle of the pastry, fold the opposite ends over the filling, and fold over the top and bottom to make a neat parcel. Repeat with the remaining sheets of fillo. Place the parcels seam-side down on a greased baking sheet, and brush them with melted butter or margarine. Bake for 30–40 minutes, until the potato parcels are golden-brown and crisp.

VEGETABLE SPRING ROLLS

MAKES ABOUT 20

25 g (1 oz) egg vermicelli
· · ·
75 g (3 oz) bean sprouts
· · ·
3 tablespoons groundnut oil
· · ·
500 g (1 lb) vegetables such as mange tout, peas, broccoli, courgettes, carrots, all cut into very small pieces
· · ·
175 g (6 oz) button mushrooms, chopped
· · ·
5 cm (2-inch) piece of root ginger, peeled and grated
· · ·
4 spring onions, chopped finely
· · ·
1–2 tablespoons soy sauce to taste
· · ·
2 tablespoons sesame oil
· · ·
500 g (1 lb) fillo pastry
· · ·
groundnut oil for deep-frying and brushing
· · ·

PREPARATION TIME: 50 MINUTES + 15 MINUTES COOKING

Soak the vermicelli in warm water while you prepare and cook the vegetables.

Steam the bean sprouts lightly over boiling water for about 5 minutes. Heat the oil in a large frying-pan with a lid, add all the prepared vegetables and the ginger and spring onions. Stir-fry them for a couple of minutes, and then stir in the soy sauce and sesame oil and leave to stand, covered but off the heat, for several minutes.

Drain the vermicelli and chop it into 6 cm (2½-inch) lengths. Mix it with the vegetables.

Take one sheet of fillo pastry with the short edge towards you, brush it with oil and fold the sheet in half. Place 2 tablespoons of the filling at one end and roll up the pastry, turning in the sides so that the filling is enclosed. Seal the edges with water. Repeat with the remaining sheets of fillo pastry.

Heat the oil to 190°C/375°F in a large deep-frying pan, add the spring rolls several at a time, turning them until they are crisp and light golden all over. Drain on kitchen paper and keep warm. Serve as soon as possible.

BUCKWHEAT BLINIS

MAKES 12–14

15 g (½ oz) dried yeast
· · ·
250 ml (8 fl oz) warm milk
· · ·
125 g (4 oz) plain flour
· · ·
150 g (5 oz) buckwheat flour
· · ·
a pinch of salt
· · ·
2 eggs, separated, plus 1 egg yolk
· · ·
250 ml (8 fl oz) soured cream or crème fraîche
· · ·
oil for greasing
· · ·

PREPARATION TIME: 15 MINUTES + 2 HOURS RISING + 30 MINUTES COOKING

These are traditional Russian fare, especially at Shrovetide. They are almost always associated with caviar, which is what the Russians like to eat them with. They are a kind of thick pancake with a lovely buckwheat flavour, and are also eaten vegetarian-style with melted butter or soured cream, or with a mixture of hard-boiled eggs in melted butter.

Mix the yeast with the warm milk and set it aside for about 10 minutes, or until frothy. Sift the flours with the salt, and then add the yeast liquid. Mix in all the egg yolks to a sticky dough. Leave the dough to rise in a warm place for 2 hours.

Beat the egg whites until stiff. Fold in the cream or crème fraîche and then the egg whites. Lightly grease a heated frying-pan and add the mixture, dropping four 1-tablespoon amounts of it into the pan at a time, to make 15 cm (6-inch) rounds, turning them until browned on both sides. Keep warm until ready to serve. Repeat with the remaining mixture until 12 blinis have been made. Serve at once.

SRI-LANKAN PUMPKIN CURRY

SERVES 4

40 g (1½ oz) desiccated coconut

• • •

450 ml (¾ pint) boiling water

• • •

3 tablespoons vegetable oil

• • •

1 large onion, chopped

• • •

1 cm (½-inch) piece of root ginger, peeled and grated

• • •

2 tablespoons medium hot curry paste

• • •

*1 kg (2 lb) pumpkin, de-seeded and cut into 5 cm (2-inch) squares
(but left unpeeled)*

• • •

1–2 green chillies, de-seeded and chopped

• • •

¼ teaspoon ground turmeric

• • •

1 cinnamon stick

• • •

2 strips of lemon zest

• • •

salt to taste

• • •

chopped coriander leaves, to garnish

• • •

PREPARATION AND COOKING TIME: 35 MINUTES + STANDING

*A hint of cinnamon and the distinctive soft flavour of coconut give
this curry its characteristic flavours. You can use any variety of squash
as well as pumpkin. Serve it with a watercress salad, basmati rice, and
some home-made Chapatis (page 120).*

Stir the coconut into the boiling water. Leave it to stand for 10 minutes before straining the coconut 'milk'.

Heat the oil in a heavy pan, and stir-fry the onion and ginger with the curry paste for about 10 minutes. Stir in the pumpkin and toss it until well coated in the oil. Add the chillies, spices, lemon zest and the strained coconut 'milk', and simmer gently for about 20 minutes or until the pumpkin is quite tender. Remove the cinnamon stick and lemon zest and season to taste with salt.

Allow the curry to stand for a while before serving – or eat it the next day since it improves with keeping. Garnish with the chopped coriander leaves.

CHAPTER FOUR

CURRIES AND STIR-FRIES

SOUTH INDIAN CURRY FEAST

| SERVES 6 |

½ small cauliflower, separated into florets
· · ·
4 tablespoons vegetable oil
· · ·
1 large onion, chopped
· · ·
375 g (12 oz) potatoes, cooked and diced
· · ·
1 green pepper, de-seeded and chopped
· · ·
2 teaspoons ground coriander
· · ·
2 teaspoons cumin seeds, toasted
· · ·
1 small chilli, de-seeded and sliced finely
· · ·
125 g (4 oz) cooked peas
· · ·
250 g (8 oz) cottage cheese
· · ·
FOR THE MUSHROOM AND LENTIL DHAL
· · ·
250 g (8 oz) green lentils, soaked for 1 hour
· · ·
4 shallots or small onions, sliced
· · ·
1 bay leaf
· · ·
1 whole chilli
· · ·
2.5 cm (1-inch) piece of root ginger, peeled and bruised
· · ·
2 teaspoons ground turmeric
· · ·
about 600 ml (1 pint) cold water
· · ·
oil for frying
· · ·
250 g (8 oz) mushrooms, halved and sliced
· · ·
2 teaspoons ground cumin
· · ·
1 teaspoon ground coriander
· · ·
salt to taste
· · ·
coriander leaves, to garnish
· · ·

PREPARATION AND COOKING TIME: 1 HOUR 35–40 MINUTES + 1 HOUR SOAKING

*F*or people who love spiced food, this dry vegetable curry, complemented by a moist dhal with mushrooms, is a real treat. The spicing is subtle rather than intrusive, and you can add finishing touches by adding a Cucumber Raita (page 43), basmati rice, Chapatis (page 120) and a salad of shredded lettuce, tomato and spring onion to complete the feast.

Lightly steam the cauliflower over boiling water for about 15 minutes, or until tender.

Heat the oil in a large saucepan, add the onion, and cook for about 10 minutes or until soft. Then add the potatoes and green pepper and toss until well coated with the oil. Stir in the spices and cook for 5 minutes, stirring occasionally. Add the remaining curry ingredients. Stir well for about 10 minutes until the ingredients are tender and the curry is ready to serve. As with all curries, its flavours improve by leaving it to stand, if possible overnight.

To make the lentil dhal, drain and rinse the lentils and put them into a saucepan with the shallots or onions, bay leaf, chilli, ginger and turmeric. Add water to just cover and bring to the boil. Cover and simmer for 25–30 minutes, until soft. The lentils will have absorbed most of the liquid but it will still be quite runny. Season to taste with salt, and allow to stand off the heat, covered, for a further 10 minutes. Heat the oil, add the mushrooms, cumin and coriander, and sauté briskly for about 5 minutes or until the mushrooms are cooked but still crisp, and then stir into the lentil mixture. Remove the bay leaf, chilli and ginger before serving garnished with fresh coriander leaves.

Chapatis (PAGE 120)
South Indian curry feast
Dry-spiced okra
Sri-Lankan pumpkin curry

COURGETTE AND CAULIFLOWER CURRY WITH CHICK-PEAS

SERVES 4–6

*250 g (8 oz) dried chick-peas, soaked overnight, or
432 g (14 oz) can of chick-peas*
• • •
about 600 ml (1 pint) vegetable stock
• • •
25 g (1 oz) butter or margarine, plus extra for greasing
• • •
1 small onion, chopped finely
• • •
1 tablespoon plain flour
• • •
2 teaspoons medium hot curry paste
• • •
1 tablespoon tomato purée
• • •
2 tablespoons smooth peanut butter
• • •
1 tablespoon soy sauce
• • •
1/2 medium-size cauliflower, separated into florets
• • •
oil for stir-frying
• • •
4 medium courgettes, cubed
• • •
300 ml (1/2 pint) natural yogurt
• • •
chopped coriander leaves, to garnish
• • •

PREPARATION TIME: 1 HOUR + SOAKING OVERNIGHT + 20 MINUTES COOKING
+ 10 MINUTES STANDING

*A nourishing combination of vegetables, this curry makes a hearty
meal which is at its best served with fried rice and a refreshing side
salad. A touch of peanut butter is added to the sauce, which is finished
with natural yogurt to balance the heat of the curry.*

Drain the dried chick-peas, cover with fresh water and simmer, covered, for about 30 minutes or until cooked. Reserve the chick-pea stock from cooking (or draining, if using canned chick-peas) and make it up to 600 ml (1 pint) using the vegetable stock. Melt the butter or margarine in a saucepan, add the onion and fry for a few minutes until softened. Sprinkle over the flour and cook, stirring, for a

*Courgette and cauliflower curry with chick-peas
Spicy sweet potatoes with cauliflower
Lentil and vegetable curry
Coconut and sweetcorn curry*

further 2–3 minutes. Mix in the curry paste, tomato purée and peanut butter and gradually add the stock, stirring. Simmer for 5 minutes; then season with the soy sauce.

Preheat the oven to Gas Mark 4/180°C/350°F. Lightly steam the cauliflower over boiling water for about 15 minutes until cooked but still crisp. Heat the oil in a frying-pan, add the courgettes and stir-fry them for about 2 minutes until cooked but crisp (*al dente*). Mix the vegetables with the chick-peas and the sauce. Grease an ovenproof dish and cover the base with the mixture. Bake for 20 minutes, and leave to stand for at least 10 minutes before stirring in the yogurt. Serve warm, sprinkled with the chopped coriander leaves.

DRY-SPICED OKRA

SERVES 4–6

1 teaspoon ground coriander
• • •
1/2 teaspoon ground turmeric
• • •
1 teaspoon garam masala powder
• • •
375 g (12 oz) okra, trimmed and cut into 5 mm (1/4-inch) slices
• • •
2 tablespoons vegetable oil
• • •
1/2 teaspoon cumin seeds
• • •
1/4 teaspoon mustard seeds
• • •
1/2 teaspoon sugar
• • •
juice of 1/2 lemon
• • •
salt to taste
• • •

PREPARATION AND COOKING TIME: 25 MINUTES

*Personally I love 'dry' curries, and often choose bhindis when I eat in
Indian restaurants. Okra make one of the finest of dry-spiced dishes, but
you can substitute cauliflower, mushrooms, potatoes, peas – and so on,
in endless variations.*

Mix the coriander, turmeric and garam masala powder in a mixing bowl and toss the okra in them until evenly coated with the spices.

Heat the oil in a wok or large frying-pan, add the cumin and mustard seeds and fry until the latter crackle. Lower the heat and add the sugar. Add the okra with the spices and stir-fry over a medium heat for 4–5 minutes or until tender. Sprinkle the lemon juice over the okra and season to taste with salt. Keep warm until ready to serve.

LENTIL AND VEGETABLE CURRY

SERVES 4

FOR THE LENTIL CURRY
· · ·
250 g (8 oz) red lentils
· · ·
2 teaspoons garam masala powder
· · ·
1/2 teaspoon ground turmeric
· · ·
about 900 ml (1 1/2 pints) cold water
· · ·
8 okra
· · ·
250 g (8 oz) cauliflower florets
· · ·
1 onion, sliced thinly
· · ·
*250 g (8 oz) mange tout or french beans, sliced into
1 cm (1/2-inch) pieces*
· · ·
2 tablespoons lemon juice
· · ·
1 teaspoon soft brown sugar
· · ·
4 tomatoes, quartered
· · ·
1 red pepper, chopped
· · ·
salt to taste
· · ·
chopped coriander leaves, to garnish
· · ·
FOR THE SPICY SAUCE
· · ·
4 tablespoons vegetable oil
· · ·
1/2 teaspoon mustard seeds
· · ·
2 whole dried chillies
· · ·
1/2 teaspoon cumin seeds
· · ·
6 curry leaves
· · ·
2 garlic cloves, crushed
· · ·
a pinch of salt
· · ·
PREPARATION AND COOKING TIME: 30 MINUTES

*K*nown *in India as* sambhar, *this simple formula can be varied with different vegetables throughout the seasons. Chopped tomatoes and peppers are added at the last minute to give the dish freshness and crunch. Serve it with basmati rice and coleslaw.*

Put the lentils, spices and water to cover into a large saucepan and bring to the boil. Lower the heat and cover the pan. Simmer for about 10–15 minutes, or until the lentils are very soft.

Add the okra, cauliflower, onion and mange tout or beans. Season with the lemon juice and sugar, and salt to taste. Add enough water to bring to the consistency of thick soup, and simmer for a further 10 minutes. Finally stir in the tomatoes and red pepper. Put aside and keep warm.

To prepare the spicy sauce, heat the oil in a small frying-pan, add all the spices and fry until the mustard seeds begin to crackle. Stand back, pour the contents of the pan over the curry, and cover immediately with a lid to seal the flavours. Garnish with coriander leaves before serving.

SPICY SWEET POTATOES WITH CAULIFLOWER

SERVES 4

4 tablespoons vegetable oil
* * *
1 large onion, sliced thinly
* * *
1 garlic clove, crushed
* * *
2.5 cm (1-inch) piece of root ginger, peeled and grated
* * *
2 teaspoons ground coriander
* * *
2 teaspoons ground cumin
* * *
2 tablespoons tomato purée
* * *
500 g (1 lb) sweet potatoes, peeled and diced
* * *
1 medium-size cauliflower, separated into florets
* * *
300 ml (½ pint) vegetable stock or water
* * *
150 g (5 oz) carton of natural yogurt
* * *
1 tablespoon finely chopped mint
* * *
salt to taste
* * *
4 hard-boiled eggs, quartered, to garnish
* * *
PREPARATION AND COOKING TIME: 40 MINUTES

Spicing sweet potato with ginger, coriander and cumin makes a delicious dish combined with cauliflower florets. Serve it either as a side vegetable or as a main course in itself, with basmati rice and puppodums or hot naan bread.

Heat the oil in a saucepan, add the onion and garlic, and cook over a gentle heat, stirring frequently, for about 5 minutes or until they are soft and translucent. Stir in the ginger, spices and tomato purée and mix well. Cook gently for 1 or 2 minutes, and then add the sweet potatoes and cauliflower and coat them with the onion and spice mixture. Add the stock or water and cover the pan tightly. Simmer gently for 10–15 minutes, stirring from time to time.

Stir in the yogurt and mint and season to taste with salt. Heat the dish through again, and then transfer it to a serving dish and garnish with the hard-boiled eggs.

CURRIED BABY AUBERGINES

SERVES 4–6

1 small onion, sliced
* * *
4 tablespoons desiccated coconut
* * *
1 teaspoon sesame seeds
* * *
1 teaspoon poppy seeds
* * *
½ teaspoon coriander seeds
* * *
5 cm (2-inch) piece of root ginger, peeled and grated
* * *
1–2 teaspoons curry paste
* * *
500 g (1 lb) baby aubergines
* * *
2 tablespoons sesame oil
* * *
2 tablespoons vegetable oil
* * *
½ teaspoon cumin seeds
* * *
salt to taste
* * *
PREPARATION TIME: 20 MINUTES + 30 MINUTES COOKING + STANDING

A delicate dish, this method of spicing young aubergines brings out the best in their texture and taste. I like to serve them with Chinese noodles.

Heat an ungreased frying-pan, add the onion, coconut and all the seeds and ginger, and dry-roast them until lightly browned. Blend in a small bowl with the curry paste.

Make two long, deep cuts along the length of each aubergine and rub a little of the paste into the incisions, reserving the rest. In a wok or large frying-pan, mix the sesame and vegetable oils and fry the cumin seeds; then add the remaining ground paste with 2–3 tablespoons water. Lower the heat, put the aubergines into the wok with a little salt and steam them, covered, for 30 minutes or until fully cooked, turning them occasionally and adding more water as necessary.

The aubergines are best eaten having been allowed to stand for 24 hours. They are delicious cold, and can be reheated very successfully.

PICTURED ON TITLE PAGE

COCONUT AND SWEETCORN CURRY

SERVES 4

1 coconut, split open

· · ·

300 ml (½ pint) hot water

· · ·

1 large mooli, peeled and sliced finely

· · ·

1 cucumber, sliced finely

· · ·

326 g (11½ oz) can of sweetcorn, drained

· · ·

2 tablespoons plain wholemeal flour

· · ·

150 g (5 oz) carton of natural yogurt

· · ·

3 tablespoons chopped coriander

· · ·

2 garlic cloves, sliced finely

· · ·

1 small chilli, sliced

· · ·

PREPARATION AND COOKING TIME: 45 MINUTES

They say in India that you should rear the coconut palm in your garden as you would rear your own son! This curry is cooked in the coconut 'milk' extracted from the nut-meat, and is a dish characteristic of southern Indian cookery. Serve this with basmati rice, Chapatis (page 120) and a side salad, or as a vegetable curry accompaniment in a more elaborate meal.

To make the coconut milk, remove the meat from the coconut, grate it and soak it in the hot water for 15 minutes. Squeeze it through a sieve to extract the coconut milk.

Put the coconut milk in a saucepan, add the mooli, cucumber and sweetcorn and cook for about 10 minutes. Beat the flour into the yogurt and add this mixture to the vegetables. Stir in the coriander, garlic and chilli and simmer for another 10 minutes.

BROCCOLI AND GINGER STIR-FRY

SERVES 3–4

750 g (1½ lb) broccoli

· · ·

2 tablespoons groundnut oil

· · ·

4 cm (1½-inch) piece of root ginger, peeled, sliced thinly and shredded or grated

· · ·

1 tablespoon soy sauce

· · ·

1 tablespoon sesame oil

· · ·

PREPARATION AND COOKING TIME: 15–20 MINUTES

This is one of my favourite supper dishes. I serve it with Chinese egg noodles, and crisp chinese leaves, bean sprouts and a tangy oriental dressing. It is simplicity itself to prepare, yet unbeatably delicious.

Separate the broccoli florets from the stems, and then slice the stems thinly.

Heat the groundnut oil in a wok or large frying-pan, add the ginger, and stir-fry over a medium heat for a few seconds. Then add the broccoli florets and stems and stir-fry for about 4 minutes until they are heated through. Add the soy sauce and sesame oil and cook for a further minute until the broccoli is cooked through. Serve hot or warm.

GOUGÈRE WITH MIXED STIR-FRIED VEGETABLES

SERVES 6

FOR THE GOUGÈRE

• • •

50 g (2 oz) butter or margarine, diced, plus extra for greasing

• • •

300 ml (½ pint) milk

• • •

125 g (4 oz) plain flour, sifted

• • •

4 eggs, beaten, plus extra to glaze

• • •

75 g (3 oz) Gruyère cheese or medium-hard cheese of your choice, diced

• • •

salt and pepper to taste

• • •

FOR THE FILLING

• • •

4 tablespoons sesame oil

• • •

2 garlic cloves, crushed

• • •

4 cm (1½-inch) piece of root ginger, peeled and grated

• • •

1 kg (2 lb) mixed vegetables, such as mushrooms, bean sprouts, courgettes, mange tout, petits pois, yellow pepper, french beans, baby carrots, cauliflower – all sliced thinly and diagonally

• • •

2–3 tablespoons soy sauce

• • •

PREPARATION AND COOKING TIME: 50–60 MINUTES

This is one of my great favourites when I am entertaining: it not only looks magnificent, but also tastes sublime. Serve it with Sauce Hollandaise (page 153) to pass around, and a glass or two of chilled white wine – and satisfaction is guaranteed!

Put the butter or margarine into a saucepan with the milk and a little salt and pepper, and bring to the boil. Add the flour and stir to a thick, smooth paste which comes away easily from the side of the pan. Remove the saucepan from the heat, cool slightly and beat in the eggs one at a time until thoroughly mixed. When the mixture is glossy and smooth, add the cheese and stir the mixture thoroughly. Check the seasoning.

Preheat the oven to Gas Mark 5/190°C/375°F. Make a ring of the mixture on a well-greased baking sheet by placing spoonfuls of the mixture in a large circle, leaving a hole in the centre and a gap between each mould of gougère so that it has room to swell. Brush with beaten egg and bake for 40–45 minutes until it is well risen and set.

To make the filling, heat the oil in a saucepan, add the garlic and ginger, and cook gently for 3–4 minutes. Increase the heat a little, add the vegetables and cook them, stirring, until they are well coated with the mixture. Add the soy sauce and continue to stir. Toss the vegetables continuously, until they are cooked through but still slightly crisp. Pile them into the centre of the gougère and serve as soon as possible.

STIR-FRIED FRENCH BEANS WITH WALNUTS

SERVES 3–4

250 ml (8 fl oz) vegetable oil

• • •

125 g (4 oz) walnut halves

• • •

500 g (1 lb) french beans, trimmed and cut diagonally into 1 cm (½-inch) pieces

• • •

2 tablespoons soy sauce or hoisin sauce

• • •

6 dried green peppercorns, ground

• • •

1 teaspoon sugar

PREPARATION AND COOKING TIME: 25 MINUTES

Deep-fried walnuts, cooked until crisp and golden, give this unusual stir-fry a delectable crunch. It makes a wonderful accompaniment to other stir-fries at a Chinese-style feast.

Heat the oil in a wok or large saucepan to 190°C/375°F, add the walnuts, and deep-fry for 60 seconds until they are golden. Lift them out with a slotted spoon and dry them on kitchen paper. When cooled, chop them coarsely.

Drain off all but 2 tablespoons of the oil, and reheat the remainder in the wok or large frying-pan until it is hot but not smoking. Stir-fry the beans for 1 minute, until they are well coated with the oil. Then add the soy or hoisin sauce, peppercorns, sugar and a little water. Cover and steam the beans over a moderate heat for 2–3 minutes until they are tender but still crisp. Add the walnuts and continue to stir-fry for another minute until they are well coated with the sauce. Season to taste with more soy sauce, and transfer to a heated serving dish.

STIR-FRY OF SUMMER VEGETABLES

SERVES 4

2 tablespoons groundnut oil

* * *

3 garlic cloves, crushed

* * *

250 g (8 oz) yellow peppers, de-seeded and sliced finely

* * *

250 g (8 oz) courgettes, sliced lengthways

* * *

250 g (8 oz) baby carrots, halved lengthways

* * *

125 ml (4 fl oz) vegetable stock

* * *

1 tablespoon rice or tarragon vinegar

* * *

2 tablespoons soy sauce

* * *

2 tablespoons finely chopped spring onions, to garnish

* * *

PREPARATION AND COOKING TIME: 25 MINUTES

You can vary the summer vegetables in this recipe according to choice: mange tout, baby broad beans and young fennel, for example, are all excellent treated in this way. Serve this stir-fry with buttered noodles.

Heat the oil in a wok or large frying-pan, add the garlic, and stir-fry over a medium heat for 30 seconds. Add the peppers, courgettes and carrots, and stir-fry for about 5 minutes or until they begin to soften. Then add the stock, vinegar and soy sauce and cover the wok. Steam the vegetables for a further 2–3 minutes, until they are tender but still crunchy.

Put the vegetables in a heated serving dish, garnish with the spring onions, and serve immediately.

PICTURED ON PAGE 11

PREVIOUS PAGE (CLOCKWISE)
Stir-fry of mange tout, mushrooms and baby corn
Stir-fried french beans with walnuts
Chinese noodles with sweet and sour stir-fry
Sauce Hollandaise (PAGE 153)
Stir-fried green beans with garlic and mushrooms
Gougère with mixed stir-fried vegetables
Broccoli and ginger stir-fry

CHINESE NOODLES WITH SWEET AND SOUR STIR-FRY

SERVES 4–6

3 tablespoons groundnut oil

* * *

2 garlic cloves, crushed

* * *

1 medium-size onion, chopped finely

* * *

1 medium-size carrot, sliced finely

* * *

2 medium-size red or green peppers, de-seeded and cut into strips

* * *

250 g (8 oz) white cabbage, shredded finely

* * *

175 g (6 oz) bean sprouts

* * *

6 radishes, sliced

* * *

175 g (6 oz) Chinese egg noodles

* * *

1–2 tablespoons sesame oil

* * *

2 tablespoons rice or cider vinegar

* * *

2 tablespoons clear honey

* * *

2 tablespoons soy sauce or black bean sauce

* * *

PREPARATION AND COOKING TIME: 20–25 MINUTES

A satisfying and tasty dish, full of flavour and texture, this stir-fry is ideal for an informal supper with friends, served with a delicate side salad of chinese leaves and radicchio.

Heat the oil in a wok or large frying-pan, add the garlic, onion, carrots and peppers, and stir-fry over a medium heat for 3–4 minutes. Add the cabbage and stir-fry for a further 3 minutes. Add the bean sprouts and radishes and stir-fry for another minute.

Meanwhile, place plenty of water in a saucepan and bring to the boil. Remove from the heat, add the noodles and leave to soak for 4–6 minutes; then drain thoroughly and toss in the sesame oil.

Mix together the vinegar, honey and soy sauce in a bowl. Pour this mixture over the vegetables, and stir until well mixed.

Make a ring of noodles around the edge of a large serving dish. Pile the vegetable stir-fry into the centre and serve immediately.

STIR-FRIED GREEN BEANS WITH GARLIC AND MUSHROOMS

SERVES 4 AS A MAIN DISH;
6–8 AS A SIDE VEGETABLE

4 tablespoons groundnut oil

• • •

3 garlic cloves, crushed

• • •

375 g (12 oz) oyster mushrooms or button mushrooms, chopped

• • •

750 g (1½ lb) young french beans, trimmed and halved

• • •

3 tablespoons vegetable stock

• • •

2 tablespoons soy sauce

• • •

2 tablespoons sesame oil

• • •

PREPARATION AND COOKING TIME: 35–40 MINUTES

The delicious flavours of garlic, soy sauce and sesame oil permeate the beans and mushrooms in this dish, which can be served either as one dish among several, or in its own right with rice or noodles, and an interesting side salad (pages 125–138).

Heat the oil in a wok or large frying-pan, add the garlic and mushrooms, and stir-fry over a medium heat for about a minute. Add the beans and stir-fry for a further 4–6 minutes until cooked through but still crisp. Add the stock, soy sauce and sesame oil, and toss the vegetables for another minute; serve immediately.

STIR-FRY OF MANGE TOUT, MUSHROOMS AND BABY CORN

SERVES 3–4

4 tablespoons groundnut oil

• • •

1 cm (½-inch) piece of root ginger, peeled and sliced very thinly

• • •

250 g (8 oz) mange tout, trimmed and sliced diagonally

• • •

250 g (8 oz) button mushrooms

• • •

175 g (6 oz) canned baby sweetcorn, drained

• • •

2 tablespoons vegetable stock

• • •

1 teaspoon sugar

• • •

1 tablespoon sesame oil

• • •

PREPARATION AND COOKING TIME: 20 MINUTES

A favourite combination, flavoured with ginger, which makes a quick, simple and delicious supper dish. I love it with Chinese noodles tossed in sesame oil with chopped spring onions, and it is also excellent with lightly buttered basmati rice.

Heat the oil in a wok or large frying-pan, add the ginger and mange tout and stir-fry for 1–2 minutes or until they soften. Add the mushrooms and stir-fry for a further minute until they absorb the oil and begin to heat through. Add the sweetcorn and stir-fry for another minute until heated through. Add the stock, sugar and sesame oil and heat through for a further minute; serve immediately.

CHAPTER FIVE

STUFFED VEGETABLES, BAKES AND GRATINS

LEEK BAKE

SERVES 4–6

750 g (1 1/2 lb) leeks, trimmed and cut in 2 cm (3/4-inch) slices
. . .
250 g (8 oz) Chinese egg noodles
. . .
300 ml (1/2 pint) Béchamel Sauce (page 158)
. . .
40 g (1 1/2 oz) vegetarian Cheddar cheese, grated finely
. . .
2 tablespoons dried breadcrumbs
. . .
15 g (1/2 oz) butter or margarine
. . .
salt and pepper to taste
. . .

PREPARATION TIME: 35 MINUTES + 15 MINUTES COOKING

Cook the leeks in boiling water or in a microwave oven, for 10 minutes or until very soft. Leave to cool; then drain.

Place the noodles in boiling water and leave for 3–4 minutes, until soft; drain thoroughly. Make layers of the leeks and noodles in a greased ovenproof dish.

Preheat the oven to Gas Mark 4/180°C/350°F. Warm the béchamel sauce over a gentle heat, add the cheese and stir until well mixed. Check the seasoning, and pour the sauce over the noodles and leeks. Sprinkle with the breadcrumbs, dot with the butter or margarine, and bake for 15 minutes.

TOMATOES WITH BASIL

SERVES 4

25 g (1 oz) butter or margarine, plus extra for greasing
. . .
1 garlic clove, cut in half
. . .
500 g (1 lb) tomatoes, sliced
. . .
3 tablespoons basil leaves
. . .
75 g (3 oz) fresh breadcrumbs, fried in oil
. . .
a little parmesan or vegetarian Cheddar cheese
. . .
salt and pepper to taste
. . .

PREPARATION TIME: 20 MINUTES + 20 MINUTES COOKING

Preheat the oven to Gas Mark 4/180°C/350°F. Grease an ovenproof dish and rub with the garlic. Cover the base with a layer of tomatoes, season and dot with a little more fat. Scatter basil on the top. Repeat alternate layers of tomatoes, butter and basil until used up; then top with the breadcrumbs. Sprinkle with the cheese and bake for 20 minutes.

SEPTEMBER STUFFED COURGETTES

> SERVES 4–6

1.1–1.25 kg (2¹/₂–3 lb) large courgettes or small marrow, trimmed

* * *

125 g (4 oz) mushrooms

* * *

175 g (6 oz) cottage cheese

* * *

75 g (3 oz) Brie, cut into 1 cm (¹/₂-inch) cubes

* * *

2 teaspoons dried mixed herbs

* * *

50 g (2 oz) watercress, chopped finely

* * *

3 tablespoons mayonnaise

* * *

2 egg yolks, beaten

* * *

salt and pepper to taste

* * *

PREPARATION TIME: 20 MINUTES + 1½ HOURS COOKING

When autumn comes with its annual glut of garden vegetables, I make variations on this theme for family meals. Stuffed large courgettes – or you can use marrow – make a wonderful supper dish served with baked potatoes and a salad of frisée lettuce and lollo rosso tossed in Vinaigrette (page 133).

Cut the courgettes or marrow in half lengthways and scoop out the seeds. Sprinkle the cut sides with salt and set aside while you prepare the stuffing.

Chop the mushrooms very finely, using a blender or food processor if possible. Mix them in a bowl with the cottage cheese, Brie, herbs, watercress and mayonnaise, and stir vigorously. Stir in the egg yolks until mixed thoroughly, and season to taste with salt and pepper.

Preheat the oven to Gas Mark 3/160°C/325°F. Wipe the cut sides of the courgettes or marrow, and pile the stuffing into the cavities. Press the two sides firmly together again and wrap securely in foil. Place in a deep baking dish and bake for about 1½ hours. Remove the foil carefully and serve the courgettes or marrow cut into thick slices.

STUFFED CABBAGE LEAVES

> SERVES 4

375 g (12 oz) mushrooms

* * *

12 large cabbage leaves

* * *

250 g (8 oz) ricotta or curd cheese

* * *

4 spring onions or shallots, chopped very finely

* * *

1 teaspoon garam masala powder (optional)

* * *

1 egg, separated

* * *

oil for greasing

* * *

6 juniper berries

* * *

1 teaspoon dried rosemary

* * *

150 ml (¹/₄ pint) vegetable stock

* * *

salt and pepper to taste

* * *

PREPARATION TIME: 35 MINUTES + 25 MINUTES COOKING

This is simple and homely food, wonderfully warming, and delicious served with rice or mashed potatoes, and a selection of vegetables in season.

Chop the mushrooms very finely, using a blender or food processor if possible. Cut the woody part out of the stem of each cabbage leaf and blanch the leaves in boiling water for 1 minute, and then refresh under cold running water and drain well. Mix the mushrooms with the ricotta or curd cheese and stir in the onions or shallots. Season to taste with salt and pepper, and add the garam masala if used. Beat the egg yolk and stir it into the mixture. Whisk the egg white until it is stiff and fold it in.

Preheat the oven to Gas Mark 5/190°C/375°F. Divide the stuffing equally between the 12 cabbage leaves, rolling each leaf into a neat parcel enclosing the stuffing. Place the cabbage leaves in an oiled shallow ovenproof dish and scatter with the juniper berries and rosemary. Moisten with the stock, cover with lightly greased foil and bake for 25 minutes. Serve hot.

VEGETABLE GARLIC CRUMBLE

SERVES 4

*750 g–1 kg (1½–2 lb) mixed vegetables of your choice, such as
carrot, cauliflower, courgette, broccoli, potato, parsnip, celery,
brussels sprouts – all peeled and trimmed*

300 ml (½ pint) Béchamel Sauce (page 158)

142 ml (¼ pint) carton of single cream

salt, pepper and grated nutmeg

FOR THE CRUMBLE

125 g (4 oz) fresh breadcrumbs

2 garlic cloves, crushed

50 g (2 oz) vegetarian Cheddar cheese, grated

25 g (1 oz) butter or margarine, diced

salt and pepper to taste

PREPARATION TIME: 30 MINUTES + 30 MINUTES COOKING

*The crumble is particularly good, being a mixture of breadcrumbs
and cheese moistened with butter or margarine and flavoured with
garlic. You can use any vegetables you like, according to season, so it is
a dish for any time of the year. In summer it is delicious with buttered
new potatoes and a side salad of feuille de chêne and cos lettuces.*

Steam the vegetables over boiling water for about 10–15
minutes, or until tender but still slightly crisp; then cut them
into bite-size pieces. Mix the béchamel sauce with the cream,
and fold it into the vegetables. Season to taste with salt,
pepper and a little nutmeg. Put the vegetable mixture in an
ovenproof dish.

Preheat the oven to Gas Mark 4/180°C/350°F. Mix the
breadcrumbs with the garlic and cheese. Add the butter or
margarine, and season to taste with salt and pepper. Spread
the mixture over the vegetables and bake for 30 minutes,
until the topping is crisp and golden. Serve hot.

Sweet and sour sauce (PAGE 155)
Stuffed cabbage leaves
Leek bake
Mushroom and lettuce gratin
Angel broccoli bake

ANGEL BROCCOLI BAKE

SERVES 4

750 g (1½ lb) broccoli, trimmed

425 g (14 oz) can of baby sweetcorn, drained

450 ml (¾ pint) Béchamel Sauce (page 158)

salt, pepper and a little ground Chinese 5-spice powder

FOR THE TOPPING

50 g (2 oz) plain flour, sifted

a pinch of salt

*1 teaspoon dried mixed herbs or
1 tablespoon finely chopped fresh parsley*

125 g (4 oz) porridge oats

75 g (3 oz) butter or margarine

25 g (1 oz) hard cheese, grated finely

50 g (2 oz) flaked almonds, toasted

salt and pepper to taste

PREPARATION TIME: 15 MINUTES + 25–30 MINUTES COOKING

*I was given this supper dish at the Angel Theatre in Bury St Edmunds
in Suffolk before we watched a show one evening. A simple but elegant
combination of broccoli and baby sweetcorn was topped with a crumbly,
nutty topping and I thought it was delicious.*

Cut the broccoli into bite-size florets and slice the stems.
Steam the broccoli over boiling water until tender but not too
soft (about 5–7 minutes). Slice the sweetcorn into 1 cm
(½-inch) lengths and mix the two vegetables with the
béchamel sauce. Season to taste with salt, pepper, and Chinese
5-spice powder and place in a large ovenproof dish.

Preheat the oven to Gas Mark 5/190°C/375°F. Sift the flour
with the salt and stir in the herbs. Add the oats, and rub in the
butter or margarine until the mixture resembles fine breadcrumbs. Stir in the cheese and almonds, and season to taste
with salt and pepper. Spread the topping over the vegetables
and bake for 25–30 minutes, until the top is golden. Serve
hot or warm.

CELERY AND NUT ROAST

SERVES 6–8

50 g (2 oz) butter or margarine, plus extra for greasing

* * *

2 large onions, chopped finely

* * *

3 large garlic cloves, crushed

* * *

1 head of celery, trimmed and sliced very finely

* * *

300 ml (½ pint) vegetable stock

* * *

1 tablespoon dried mixed Provençal herbs

* * *

a small bunch of parsley, chopped finely

* * *

grated zest of 2 lemons

* * *

juice of 1 lemon

* * *

250 g (8 oz) flaked almonds, toasted

* * *

125 g (4 oz) cashew or brazil nuts, chopped

* * *

125 g (4 oz) porridge oats

* * *

3 eggs, beaten

* * *

175 g (6 oz) vegetarian Cheddar cheese, grated finely

* * *

4 large tomatoes, sliced

* * *

salt and pepper to taste

PREPARATION TIME: 30 MINUTES + 50–55 MINUTES COOKING
+ 15–20 MINUTES STANDING

Generally speaking I feel that the nut-roast theme in vegetarian cooking is overdone, but this one is so scrumptious, so unashamedly rich and full of flavour, that it deserves to be included. Serve it with a sauce of your choice (pages 152–158) and Salad Bagration (page 130).

Melt the butter or margarine in a saucepan, add the onions, garlic and celery, and sauté for 5 minutes. Add the stock and simmer for a further 5 minutes; then stir in all the herbs, and the lemon zest and juice. Remove the pan from the heat, reserve 2 tablespoons of the nuts, and stir in the remaining nuts together with the oats. Season to taste with salt and pepper and bind with the beaten eggs.

Preheat the oven to Gas Mark 3/160°C/325°F. Place half the mixture in a well-greased 1.5 kg (3½ lb) loaf tin. Cover with the cheese and a layer of the tomatoes, reserving a few for the top. Cover with the remaining nut mixture and decorate with the remaining tomato slices. Sprinkle with the reserved nuts. Cover with foil and bake for 45 minutes. Remove the foil and cook for a further 5–10 minutes to brown the top a little.

Leave the nut roast to stand in the tin for 15–20 minutes before you attempt to turn it out. Serve warm or cold, cut into thick slices.

RUSSIAN POTATO AND MUSHROOM BAKE

SERVES 4–6

4 tablespoons olive oil

* * *

2 large onions, sliced finely

* * *

250 g (8 oz) mushrooms, sliced

* * *

1 tablespoon chopped dill

* * *

1 tablespoon chopped parsley

* * *

375 g (12 oz) potatoes, peeled and sliced thinly

* * *

450 ml (¾ pint) milk

* * *

salt and pepper and a little ground cumin

PREPARATION TIME: 30 MINUTES + 1¼ HOURS COOKING

A Russian friend described this dish to me with such enthusiasm that I had no alternative but to try it out. She was right: it is lovely, especially served with Red and White Salad with Watercress (page 128).

Heat the oil in a large frying-pan, add the onions, and fry gently over a medium heat for about 4–5 minutes, or until they soften. Cover the pan with a lid or foil and continue to cook over a very low heat, stirring from time to time, for a further 15 minutes, or until the onions are completely soft and sweet.

Preheat the oven to Gas Mark 3/160°C/325°F. Stir the mushrooms into the onions and mix until well coated in the oil. Add the herbs and season to taste with salt, pepper and cumin. Place a layer of the potatoes in a shallow ovenproof dish, cover with the mushroom mixture and finish with an overlapping layer of potatoes on top. Pour over the milk and bake for 1¼ hours, or until all the milk has been absorbed.

CAULIFLOWER BAKE POLONAISE

> **SERVES 4–6**

1 large cauliflower, separated into florets
· · ·
1 bay leaf
· · ·
3 tablespoons olive oil
· · ·
5 medium-size courgettes, sliced
· · ·
1 onion, sliced thinly
· · ·
1 tablespoon chopped tarragon
· · ·
5 large mushrooms, halved and sliced
· · ·
15 g (½ oz) arrowroot
· · ·
4 medium-size tomatoes, peeled and chopped
· · ·
FOR THE POLONAISE TOPPING
· · ·
175 g (6 oz) dried wholemeal breadcrumbs
· · ·
4 hard-boiled eggs, chopped finely
· · ·
a large bunch of parsley, chopped finely
· · ·
50 g (2 oz) butter or margarine, softened
· · ·
salt and pepper to taste

PREPARATION TIME: 45 MINUTES + 30–35 MINUTES COOKING

*F*lorets of cauliflower and slices of courgette are coated in a tarragon-flavoured tomato sauce and topped with a buttery coating of breadcrumbs, chopped hard-boiled egg and parsley. A lovely supper dish served with small potatoes and Exotic Salad (page 133).

Lightly cook the cauliflower with the bay leaf for about 15 minutes, or until tender but not too soft. Remove from the liquid and put to one side, reserving the cooking liquid.

Heat the oil in a saucepan, stir in the courgettes, onion and tarragon and cook for about 5 minutes or until the onion is soft. Add the mushrooms and stir-fry for a further 3–4 minutes until they are coated with oil and beginning to soften. Add 150 ml (¼ pint) of the reserved cooking liquid and bring to simmering point.

Mix the arrowroot with a little cold water and add it to the pan, stirring constantly until the mixture thickens. Season to taste with salt and pepper, add the tomatoes and simmer for 5 minutes. Put the mixture in a large ovenproof dish, and place the cauliflower on top.

Preheat the oven to Gas Mark 4/180°C/350°F. To prepare the Polonaise topping, mix together the breadcrumbs, eggs and parsley, and season to taste with salt and pepper. Spread the topping over the cauliflower, dot with the butter or margarine, and bake for 30–35 minutes, or until well browned and crisp.

MUSHROOM AND LETTUCE GRATIN

> **SERVES 4**

2 medium-size iceberg or crisp lettuces, trimmed and shredded
· · ·
375 g (12 oz) button mushrooms, quartered
· · ·
300 ml (½ pint) Béchamel Sauce (page 158)
· · ·
142 ml (¼ pint) carton of single cream
· · ·
2 tablespoons chopped chives
· · ·
2 tablespoons chopped marjoram
· · ·
50 g (2 oz) fresh breadcrumbs
· · ·
oil for frying
· · ·

PREPARATION TIME: 10–15 MINUTES + 15 MINUTES COOKING

*L*ettuce becomes a deliciously original vegetable when it is lightly cooked, and is well complemented in this dish by the mushrooms which are also lightly cooked. The vegetables are topped with a creamy sauce aromatic with herbs, and finished with a sprinkling of fried breadcrumbs. This makes a lovely meal served with new potatoes and some warm Sage Bread (page 122) to mop up the juices.

Preheat the oven to Gas Mark 5/190°C/375°F. Cover the base of a shallow ovenproof dish with the lettuce, and place the mushrooms on top. Heat the béchamel sauce gently, and stir in the cream until well mixed. Stir in the herbs and pour this sauce over the mushrooms. Bake for 15 minutes.

Meanwhile, fry the breadcrumbs in the oil until they are golden and crisp. Drain them thoroughly on kitchen paper. Sprinkle them over the top of the vegetable gratin and serve at once.

STUFFED AUBERGINES PROVENÇALE

> SERVES 6

6 small—medium aubergines, stalks removed

* * *

125 ml (4 fl oz) olive oil

* * *

4 large onions, chopped finely

* * *

a bunch of parsley, chopped

* * *

4 garlic cloves, chopped finely

* * *

1 kg (2 lb) ripe tomatoes, skinned and chopped

* * *

125 ml (4 fl oz) cold water

* * *

salt and pepper to taste

* * *

PREPARATION TIME: 30 MINUTES + 45–60 MINUTES COOKING

These aubergines are sliced lengthways and filled with a classic mixture of sautéd onion, parsley and garlic, and then they are steamed with chopped tomatoes over a very low heat until they are succulent. The aubergines are delicious hot, warm or cold.

Make three deep lengthways slits in each aubergine, sprinkle with salt and set aside.

Heat the oil in a saucepan, add the onions, and stir gently for about 10 minutes until they become slightly sweet. Stir in the parsley and garlic and cook for a further 5 minutes. Wipe the aubergines and use this mixture to stuff the slits in the aubergines, using any excess to cover the aubergines as a topping. Place the aubergines in a large flameproof casserole dish, cover them with the tomatoes and season to taste with salt and pepper. Sprinkle with the water and cover the casserole tightly. Cook over the gentlest of heats for 45 minutes–1 hour, turning the aubergines from time to time, and replenishing the water as necessary. Serve hot, warm or cold.

PREVIOUS PAGE (CLOCKWISE)
Vegetable garlic crumble
Tomatoes with basil
Aubergine and rosemary casserole
Sauce fines herbes (PAGE 154)
Cauliflower layer bake
September stuffed courgettes
Celery and nut roast
Vegetable terrine

VEGETABLE TERRINE

> SERVES 6–8

375 g (12 oz) cauliflower, separated into florets

* * *

2 tablespoons chopped coriander

* * *

6 eggs, beaten well

* * *

500 g (1 lb) carrots, peeled and sliced

* * *

5 tablespoons single cream

* * *

1 teaspoon ground ginger

* * *

500 g (1 lb) mushrooms

* * *

butter or margarine for greasing

* * *

salt, pepper and grated nutmeg

* * *

coriander leaves, to garnish

* * *

PREPARATION TIME: 45 MINUTES + 45 MINUTES COOKING + 15 MINUTES STANDING

An elegant dish for special occasions, this loaf is subtly flavoured and lovely to look at with its stripes of three different colours. Serve it with a sauce of your choice (pages 152–158), a potato dish and Chinese Carrot and Coriander Salad (page 130).

Lightly cook the cauliflower in boiling water for about 15 minutes, or until tender; drain and blend smoothly to a purée with a little of the cooking liquid. Season to taste with salt and pepper and stir in the coriander. Stir in 2 of the eggs.

Cook the carrots in boiling water for about 20 minutes, or until soft; drain and blend smoothly with half the cream. Stir in 2 of the eggs and season to taste with salt, pepper and the ground ginger.

Blend the mushrooms smoothly until very finely chopped. Stir in the remaining cream and eggs. Season with salt, pepper and a little nutmeg.

Preheat the oven to Gas Mark 6/200°C/400°F. Grease a 1 kg (2 lb) loaf tin and spread the cauliflower purée evenly over the base. Cover with the carrot purée and finish with the mushroom purée. Stand the loaf tin in a roasting tin of hot water about 3–5 cm (1–2 inches) deep and bake for about 45 minutes. Leave the terrine to stand on a wire rack for at least 15 minutes before you attempt to turn it out. Eat warm or cold garnished with coriander leaves.

SOUFFLÉ JACKET POTATOES

SERVES 4

2 large baking potatoes
. . .
25 g (1 oz) butter or margarine
. . .
2 tablespoons mayonnaise
. . .
175 g (6 oz) cottage cheese
. . .
2 teaspoons dried mixed herbs
. . .
125 g (4 oz) vegetarian Cheddar cheese, grated finely
. . .
1 teaspoon garam masala powder
. . .
2 teaspoons coarse-grain mustard
. . .
a small bunch of parsley, chopped
. . .
2 eggs, separated
. . .
salt and pepper to taste
. . .
chopped parsley, to garnish
. . .

PREPARATION TIME: 15 MINUTES + 1½–1¾ HOURS COOKING

Wonderful family food in cold weather, these soufflé-stuffed potatoes look fabulous, too, and make a complete meal served with grilled tomatoes and a tossed side salad of watercress and lettuce.

Preheat the oven to Gas Mark 6/200°C/400°F. Bake the potatoes for 1 hour. Allow them to cool a little; then cut in half lengthways. Carefully spoon out the flesh leaving a 5 mm (¼-inch) shell of potato skin.

Lower the oven temperature to Gas Mark 5/190°C/375°F. Mash the potato flesh with the butter or margarine, and mix with the mayonnaise and cottage cheese. Stir in the herbs, three-quarters of the Cheddar cheese, the garam masala, mustard and parsley, and season to taste with salt and pepper. Mix thoroughly, then beat in the egg yolks. Beat the egg whites stiffly and fold them in; then pile the filling into the potato shells. Sprinkle with the remaining cheese and bake for a further 25–30 minutes, or until the filling is risen and golden. Sprinkle with chopped parsley and serve.

CAULIFLOWER LAYER BAKE

SERVES 4–6

1 medium-size cauliflower, separated into florets
. . .
300 ml (½ pint) Béchamel Sauce (page 158)
. . .
125 g (4 oz) vegetarian Cheddar cheese, grated finely
. . .
250 g (8 oz) cooked basmati rice
. . .
375 g (12 oz) button mushrooms, sliced
. . .
50 g (2 oz) fresh breadcrumbs
. . .
3 tablespoons sesame seeds
. . .
40 g (1½ oz) butter or margarine, diced
. . .
salt and pepper to taste
. . .

PREPARATION TIME: 30 MINUTES + 20–25 MINUTES COOKING

I love this bake for its delicate flavours, yet it has an earthy, satisfying quality. It's a useful stand-by, being very simple to prepare, and is good served with Indonesian Salad (page 132).

Lightly steam the cauliflower over boiling water for about 10 minutes, or until tender but not too soft. Heat the béchamel sauce gently, add half of the cheese and stir until it melts. Fold the cauliflower into the sauce and season to taste with salt and pepper. Cover the base of a 20 cm (8-inch) soufflé dish with a layer of cooked rice, followed by the mushrooms and finally the cauliflower sauce.

Preheat the oven to Gas Mark 4/180°C/350°F. Mix the breadcrumbs with the sesame seeds and the remaining cheese and fold in the butter or margarine. Sprinkle the topping over the cauliflower and bake for 20–25 minutes, or until the topping is golden-brown and crisp.

MUSHROOM MOUSSAKA WITH ALMONDS

SERVES 6

2 large aubergines, sliced
· · ·
3 tablespoons olive oil, plus extra for greasing
· · ·
1 large onion, chopped
· · ·
2 garlic cloves, crushed
· · ·
2 large courgettes, diced
· · ·
500 g (1 lb) flat mushrooms, diced
· · ·
2 bay leaves
· · ·
2 tablespoons dried mixed Provençal herbs
· · ·
397 g (14 oz) can of tomatoes
· · ·
250 g (8 oz) almonds, toasted
· · ·
600 ml (1 pint) Béchamel Sauce (page 158)
· · ·
75 g (3 oz) vegetarian Cheddar cheese, grated finely
· · ·
3 eggs
· · ·
50 g (2 oz) flaked almonds
· · ·
salt and pepper to taste

PREPARATION TIME: 40 MINUTES + 40–45 MINUTES COOKING

Serve this special moussaka with new potatoes or noodles, and a tossed salad of iceberg lettuce, watercress and sliced yellow peppers.

Preheat the oven to Gas Mark 3/160°C/325°F. Liberally oil 2 large baking sheets, and place the aubergine slices on them. Brush the aubergines liberally with more oil, and bake for 20 minutes, turning them over after the first 10 minutes.

Heat the olive oil in a saucepan, add the onion, and sauté gently for about 5 minutes, or until it turns transparent. Stir in the garlic, courgettes, mushrooms, bay leaves and herbs, and cook until the vegetables are soft and well mixed. Add the tomatoes with their juice, cover the pan and simmer for a further 5 minutes. Season to taste with salt and pepper and remove the bay leaves.

Cover the base of a large ovenproof dish with layers of the vegetable mixture, followed by the aubergine slices and finally the almonds.

Increase the oven temperature to Gas Mark 4/180°C/350°F. Heat the béchamel sauce and stir in the cheese until it melts. Beat the eggs and fold them into the sauce. Cover the almond layer with the béchamel sauce and scatter the flaked almonds on top. Bake for 40–45 minutes, or until the topping is golden. Eat hot, warm or cold.

Cauliflower bake Polonaise
Mushroom moussaka with almonds
Stuffed aubergines Provençale
Russian potato and mushroom bake
Soufflé jacket potatoes

AUBERGINE AND ROSEMARY CASSEROLE

SERVES 4

2 large aubergines, sliced thinly
· · ·
4 large tomatoes, sliced thinly
· · ·
2 large onions, chopped finely
· · ·
4 tablespoons chopped rosemary, or
2 tablespoons dried rosemary
· · ·
4 tablespoons olive oil, plus extra for greasing
· · ·
125 g (4 oz) vegetarian Cheddar cheese, grated
· · ·
6 tablespoons fresh breadcrumbs, fried in oil
· · ·
salt and pepper to taste
· · ·

PREPARATION TIME: 40 MINUTES + 1 HOUR COOKING

This robust dish, which can be served as a main course in its own right, has two distinctly Mediterranean tastes – the dense flavour of aubergines and highly aromatic rosemary – which combine to make a dish that seems full of summer. Serve it with pasta tossed in olive oil.

Sprinkle the aubergine slices with salt and leave them to sweat for 30 minutes. Preheat the oven to Gas Mark 3/160°C/325°F. Rinse the aubergine slices and pat dry. Grease a 1.5-litre (2½-pint) ovenproof dish. Cover the base with layers of aubergine and tomatoes, sprinkled with chopped onion, rosemary and oil, and season to taste with salt and pepper. Mix the cheese and breadcrumbs and spread them over the top of the casserole. Bake in the oven for 1 hour and serve warm.

CHAPTER SIX

VEGETABLES AS SIDE DISHES AND STARTERS

GARLIC MUSHROOMS

SERVES 4

8 medium-size flat mushrooms
. . .
50 g (2 oz) butter or margarine, plus extra for greasing
. . .
3 celery sticks, chopped finely
. . .
2 tablespoons chopped parsley
. . .
2 large garlic cloves, crushed
. . .
200 g (7 oz) round goat cheese
. . .
salt and pepper to taste
. . .
watercress sprigs, to garnish
. . .

PREPARATION TIME: 20 MINUTES + 15 MINUTES COOKING

Large flat mushrooms, filled with crunchy celery, parsley and garlic, and topped with melting cheese, make an irresistible starter – or even a light meal in their own right, served on a bed of lettuce with Wholemeal Bread (page 121) or Sesame Pitta Bread (page 117).

Remove the mushroom stalks and chop them finely. Melt the butter or margarine in a saucepan, add the celery, and cook over a gentle heat for about 5 minutes, or until softened. Add the mushroom stalks and cook for a further 3–4 minutes until they are soft. Stir in the parsley and garlic, and season to taste with salt and pepper.

Preheat the oven to Gas Mark 5/190°C/375°F. Cover the mushroom caps with the mixture and press it down firmly. Place in a lightly oiled shallow ovenproof dish, and cover each mushroom with a slice of cheese. Bake for 15 minutes. Serve immediately, garnished with a sprig or two of watercress.

CELERIAC REMOULADE

SERVES 4

250 g (8 oz) celeriac, peeled
* * *
juice of ½ lemon
* * *
25 g (1 oz) capers
* * *
25 g (1 oz) gherkin, chopped
* * *
150 g (5 oz) Mayonnaise (page 158)
* * *
25 g (1 oz) Dijon mustard
* * *
PREPARATION TIME: 15 MINUTES

A French classic, this is a winter favourite of mine. Grated celeriac is dressed in a mustardy mayonnaise with capers and gherkins added.

Grate the celeriac coarsely. Place it in cold water with the lemon juice to prevent it discolouring while you prepare the sauce.

Chop the capers with the gherkins so finely that they are practically mashed. Stir these into the mayonnaise, add the mustard and mix well.

Drain the celeriac thoroughly and dry it. Mix it with the mayonnaise until completely coated.

JUNIPER POTATOES

SERVES 2–3

500 g (1 lb) waxy potatoes, peeled and grated coarsely
* * *
25 g (1 oz) butter or margarine, plus extra for greasing
* * *
1 tablespoon sunflower oil
* * *
8 juniper berries, crushed
* * *
salt and pepper to taste
* * *
PREPARATION AND COOKING TIME: 40–50 MINUTES

Of all the ways to cook potatoes, this, to me, is the best. The potatoes, without their excess starch, are really delicate in flavour, and the subtle taste of juniper makes this a side dish to remember. You can also use it as a base for fried eggs, to make a delicious supper dish.

Soak the potatoes in cold water for 5 minutes to remove the excess starch; then rinse them very well, drain and dry them thoroughly on kitchen paper. Melt the butter or margarine in a heavy non-stick saucepan, add the oil, and then toss in the potatoes, turning them until they are well coated in the fat. As the potatoes begin to soften, season to taste with salt and pepper, and add the juniper berries. Lower the heat very low and cover the pan with a sheet of greased foil and a lid. Cook for 30–40 minutes; then increase the heat for a few minutes until the potatoes are crisp and brown underneath. Grill the top briefly, and then turn them out on to a hot plate to serve.

HARICOTS VERTS AU FROMAGE

SERVES 3–4

375 g (12 oz) fine green beans, trimmed
* * *
50 g (2 oz) Gruyère or other medium-hard cheese of your choice, diced
* * *
a small bunch of tarragon, chopped finely
* * *
5 tablespoons Vinaigrette (page 133)
* * *
PREPARATION AND COOKING TIME: 15 MINUTES + STANDING

This salad, pungent with tarragon, is lovely as a starter served with Melba toast, or as part of a buffet table.

Cook the beans for about 5–7 minutes, or until they are cooked through but still firm (*al dente*); drain them and refresh under cold running water. When cold, drain well and mix them thoroughly with the cheese, tarragon and vinaigrette. Allow the salad to stand for a while at room temperature before serving.

SWEET POTATOES CARIBBEAN-STYLE

SERVES 4–6

4 tablespoons vegetable oil

• • •

1 tablespoon fenugreek seeds

• • •

2 garlic cloves, sliced

• • •

1 tablespoon garam masala paste

• • •

1 kg (2 lb) sweet potatoes, peeled and sliced

• • •

salt to taste

• • •

PREPARATION AND COOKING TIME: 25 MINUTES

Sweet potatoes makes a delightful side vegetable lightly spiced with garam masala and garlic. The addition of fenugreek gives this dish an ethnic quality.

Heat the oil in a saucepan, add the fenugreek and garlic, and fry until the garlic is light brown. Lift them out with a slotted spoon and discard. Add the garam masala to the oil, reduce the heat and stir for 3–4 minutes; then stir in the sweet potatoes. Season to taste with salt, and stir-fry until the potatoes are well coated with the oil. Add a little water, cover the pan, and simmer very gently for 10–12 minutes, turning the potatoes once. Add more water if necessary, to prevent the sweet potatoes from sticking to the pan – but the finished dish should be dry and the potatoes tender.

GRILLED LEEKS TAHINA

SERVES 4

8 medium-size leeks, cut into 2.5 cm (1-inch) pieces

• • •

4 tablespoons sesame oil

• • •

1–2 tablespoons tahina paste

• • •

5 tablespoons french dressing

• • •

2 tablespoons sesame seeds, toasted, to garnish

• • •

PREPARATION AND COOKING TIME: 15 MINUTES + COOLING

This very unusual treatment of leeks makes a sensational hors d'oeuvre. The leeks are first lightly blanched, and then grilled with sesame oil and dressed in a vinaigrette flavoured with tahina paste. The final touch of toasted sesame seeds gives the dish a crunchy finish.

Blanch the leeks in boiling water until soft but firm. Drain; then grill the leeks under a moderate heat, brushing them with sesame oil and turning them until they are lightly browned and tender. Keep the heat low to prevent them from burning. Leave them to cool. Thoroughly mix the tahina paste with the french dressing and toss the leeks in this; set them aside until cold. Serve them sprinkled with the toasted sesame seeds.

CREAMY BROCCOLI PURÉE

SERVES 4

750 g (1½ lb) broccoli

• • •

15 g (½ oz) hard cheese, grated finely

• • •

5–6 tablespoons single cream

• • •

grated nutmeg and salt to taste

• • •

PREPARATION AND COOKING TIME: 15 MINUTES

I love vegetable purées as winter food. Broccoli, brussels sprouts, carrots, cauliflower and celeriac – there are endless variations on this theme and they are all delicious in their own way. If possible, use a microwave to make this dish as the broccoli retains its flavour better using this form of cooking.

Steam the broccoli over boiling water for about 8–10 minutes until cooked through and the stems are completely soft. Leave to cool, and reserve the cooking liquid.

Blend the cooled broccoli with enough of the reserved cooking liquid to make a fairly thick purée. Stir in the cheese and cream, and season to taste with nutmeg and salt. Reheat the purée gently and serve.

Celeriac remoulade
Haricot verts au fromage
Deep-fried 'seaweed'
Juniper potatoes
Garlic mushrooms

SCALLOPED POTATOES

SERVES 6

750 g (1½ lb) medium-size potatoes, peeled

• • •

284 ml (½ pint) carton of single cream

• • •

butter or margarine for greasing

• • •

salt, pepper and freshly grated ground nutmeg to taste

• • •

PREPARATION TIME: 15 MINUTES + 1¼–1½ HOURS COOKING

A lovely way of cooking potatoes slowly to bring out the subtlety of their flavour, this creamy, satisfying dish goes very well with many vegetarian main courses. You could try adding polenta (coarse corn meal) to ring the changes.

Preheat the oven to Gas Mark 4/180°C/350°F. Slice the potatoes very thinly, if possible using the slicer of a food processor. Heat the cream to boiling point. Grease a shallow ovenproof 25 cm (10-inch) dish and cover the base with a layer of potatoes, sprinkling each layer with salt, pepper and nutmeg, and spooning 3–4 tablespoons hot cream over each one. Finish the top layer with all the remaining cream. Cover with foil and bake in the lower section of the oven for 1¼–1½ hours, removing the foil for the last 30–40 minutes to allow the potatoes on top to brown.

SUMMER SQUASH 'COCKAIGNE'

SERVES 4

750 g (1½ lb) summer squash, skinned, de-seeded and diced

• • •

4 tablespoons soured cream

• • •

40 g (1½ oz) butter or margarine

• • •

25 g (1 oz) vegetarian Cheddar cheese, grated

• • •

2 egg yolks, beaten

• • •

1 tablespoon chopped chives

• • •

40 g (1½ oz) dried wholemeal breadcrumbs

• • •

salt and paprika

• • •

PREPARATION TIME: 30 MINUTES + 15 MINUTES COOKING

The delightful sight of all the different squashes in late summer is an inspiration in itself to any cook. There are countless ways of cooking squashes, and this is a traditional American recipe that does summer squash full justice.

Place the squash in enough water to cover and simmer for 6–8 minutes or until tender. Drain; then stir in the cream, 15 g (½ oz) of the butter or margarine, and the cheese, and mix thoroughly until the cheese has melted. Season to taste with salt and paprika.

Preheat the oven to Gas Mark 5/190°C/375°F. Stir in the egg yolks and chives, and put the mixture in a 900 ml (1½-pint) ovenproof dish. Cover with the breadcrumbs, dot with the remaining butter or margarine, and bake for 15 minutes.

ARTICHOKES FRIED WITH GARLIC BUTTER

SERVES 4

750 g (1½ lb) jerusalem artichokes, peeled

• • •

50 g (2 oz) butter or margarine

• • •

2 large garlic cloves, crushed

• • •

salt and pepper to taste

• • •

1 tablespoon finely chopped parsley, to garnish

• • •

PREPARATION TIME: 20 MINUTES

This recipe is among the finest of winter dishes: it is as delicious as it is satisfying; it smells really tempting; and it lingers on the taste-buds. Serve it with a simple main course, and a basket of fresh bread to mop up the garlicky juices.

Cook the artichokes in boiling water for about 10 minutes, or until they are cooked through but still firm (*al dente*). Cut them into small cubes. Melt the butter or margarine in a saucepan, add the artichokes and fry, tossing them until they are golden all over. Lower the heat and stir in the garlic, mixing thoroughly. Season to taste with salt and pepper, transfer the mixture to a warm serving dish, and serve sprinkled with the parsley.

CHICORY À LA GRECQUE

SERVES 4

2.25 litres (4 pints) water
· · ·
150 ml (¼ pint) olive oil
· · ·
10 coriander seeds
· · ·
10 black peppercorns
· · ·
1 large bouquet of dried herbs or
2 bouquet garni sachets
· · ·
juice of 2 lemons
· · ·
8 medium-size heads of chicory
· · ·
salt to taste

PREPARATION AND COOKING TIME: 40 MINUTES + SEVERAL HOURS COOLING

Chicory has been used in salads since ancient times, although some varieties are cultivated for their large roots, which when dried, roasted and ground are blended with coffee. When used as a food plant, chicory is blanched to reduce its bitterness and is as good cooked as it is raw in salads.

Simmer the water with the oil, spices, salt to taste, herbs and lemon juice for 10 minutes.

Meanwhile, plunge the chicory into boiling water, cook it for 2 minutes and then remove. This initial blanching reduces the bitterness of the vegetable when cooked. Add the chicory to the liquid and simmer for a further 20 minutes. Allow it to cool in the liquid.

When the chicory is cold, place it in a serving dish. Boil the remaining liquid down hard to reduce it to 300 ml (½ pint) and then cool it and pour over the chicory. Serve chilled, either as an hors d'oeuvre or as a side salad.

AUBERGINES FRITES AUX FINES HERBES

SERVES 4

2 aubergines
· · ·
vegetable oil for frying
· · ·
5–6 tablespoons milk
· · ·
50 g (2 oz) plain flour
· · ·
a bunch of parsley, chives and tarragon, chopped finely
· · ·
salt
· · ·

PREPARATION AND COOKING TIME: 25 MINUTES + 30 MINUTES SALTING

I think this is one of the best ways of cooking aubergines. Based on a classic French recipe, the peeled strips of aubergine are lightly coated in milk and flour, and fried in very hot oil.

Peel the aubergines and cut them lengthways in long strips. Sprinkle with salt, leave for 30 minutes, rinse and pat dry. Heat the oil in a saucepan to 190°C/375°F. Dip each aubergine slice in the milk and draw it through the flour; then plunge into the very hot oil. Deep-fry until the aubergine slices are golden all over; then drain on kitchen paper and sprinkle with salt. Put the aubergine in a warm serving dish, sprinkle with the chopped herbs and serve as soon as possible.

FOLLOWING PAGE (CLOCKWISE)
Chicory à la Grecque
Summer squash 'Cockaigne'
Creamy broccoli purée
Scalloped potatoes
Sauce printanier (PAGE 153)
Aubergine frites aux fine herbes
Artichokes fried with garlic butter
Sesame parsnips

SESAME PARSNIPS

SERVES 6

150 ml (¼ pint) vegetable oil

• • •

50 g (2 oz) sesame seeds

• • •

3 tablespoons soy sauce

• • •

1 kg (2 lb) parsnips, peeled

• • •

PREPARATION TIME: 10 MINUTES + 15–20 MINUTES COOKING

Roast parsnips are one of the good things about winter. Add some sesame seeds, and a seasoning of soy sauce, and this treat becomes yet more memorable.

Preheat the oven to Gas Mark 7/220°C/425°F. Put the oil in a large baking dish or roasting tin and heat for a few minutes in the oven. Stir in the sesame seeds and then the soy sauce and mix well. Slice the parsnips lengthways into strips and add them to the hot oil mixture. Roast the parsnips for 15–20 minutes, turning once or twice, until lightly browned on the outside and soft inside.

BUTTERED CABBAGE WITH ROSEMARY

SERVES 4

500 g (1 lb) white cabbage, sliced finely

• • •

1 tablespoon finely chopped rosemary or 2 teaspoons dried rosemary

• • •

75 g (3 oz) butter or margarine

• • •

pepper to taste

• • •

PREPARATION AND COOKING TIME: 10 MINUTES

The flavour of rosemary stands out beautifully in contrast to nut brown butter, which is poured over the cooked cabbage just before serving.

Cook the cabbage in boiling water for 5–8 minutes, until tender but still slightly crisp. Drain it, mix in the rosemary and keep it warm. Melt the butter or margarine in a small saucepan and cook until it turns nut-brown. Pour over the cabbage and toss thoroughly. Season to taste with pepper, toss again, and serve.

MASHED WINTER SQUASH

SERVES 6–8

1.5–2 kg (3½–4½ lb) winter squash, skinned, de-seeded and chopped

• • •

40 g (1½ oz) butter or margarine

• • •

3 teaspoons brown sugar

• • •

1 teaspoon ground ginger

• • •

2 tablespoons freshly squeezed orange juice

• • •

4–5 tablespoons double cream

• • •

15 g (1 oz) shelled walnuts, chopped finely

• • •

PREPARATION TIME: 10 MINUTES + 20–25 MINUTES COOKING

The squash in this warming recipe is mashed with a little sugar, ginger and orange juice, and thinned out with cream. A sprinkling of crunchy walnuts on top offers a delectable contrast of texture to the soft mashed vegetable.

Preheat the oven to Gas Mark 5/190°C/375°F. Place the squash in a 2-litre (3½-pint) ovenproof dish with a little water, cover with foil and bake for about 20–25 minutes, until soft. Drain and cool.

Put the squash into a saucepan and mash it with the butter or margarine, sugar, ginger and orange juice. Add enough cream to mix to a good consistency, heat the mixture through and place it in a serving dish. Sprinkle with the chopped walnuts.

Steamed tamari mushrooms
Grilled leeks tahina
Buttered cabbage with rosemary
Sweet potatoes Caribbean-style
Mashed winter squash

STEAMED TAMARI MUSHROOMS

SERVES 3–4

1 tablespoon sunflower oil

• • •

1 garlic clove, crushed

• • •

2 tablespoons sesame seeds

• • •

500 g (1 lb) small button mushrooms

• • •

2 tablespoons soy sauce

• • •

2 tablespoons sesame oil

• • •

1 tablespoon black bean sauce

• • •

PREPARATION AND COOKING TIME: 15 MINUTES

I make these mushrooms regularly, sometimes as a starter for an informal meal, but more often as one of two or three light vegetable dishes for supper. They are so easy to prepare, and so delicious, that I never tire of them.

Heat the oil in a saucepan, add the garlic and sesame seeds, and sauté for 1–2 minutes. Add the mushrooms, and cook, stirring for a minute; then cover the pan, and cook over a low heat for a further 10 minutes or until the mushrooms are quite tender. Stir in the soy sauce, cook for a further minute, then transfer immediately to a serving dish. Mix the sesame oil with the black bean sauce, stir them into the mushrooms and serve. This is lovely hot, warm or cold.

DEEP-FRIED 'SEAWEED'

SERVES 4

6 medium-size green cabbage leaves

• • •

vegetable oil for deep-frying

• • •

salt if necessary

• • •

PREPARATION AND COOKING TIME: 10 MINUTES

One of life's surprises is how cabbage changes and develops its flavour when it is deep-fried. Known in Chinese cuisine as 'seaweed', it makes a delectable starter to an oriental-style meal.

Using a very sharp knife, shred the cabbage leaves very finely indeed. Heat the oil in a large saucepan to 190°C/375°F, add the cabbage, and deep-fry for a minute or so until darkened and crisp. Lift out the cabbage and drain it on kitchen paper. Sprinkle with a little salt if used, and the dish is ready to serve.

CHAPTER SEVEN

PASTA

FARFALLE WITH BASIL AND COURGETTES

| SERVES 4 |

375 g (12 oz) pasta bows

• • •

4 tablespoons olive oil

• • •

250 g (8 oz) small courgettes, sliced thinly

• • •

175 g (6 oz) button mushrooms, sliced

• • •

2 garlic cloves, crushed

• • •

3 tablespoons chopped basil

• • •

salt and pepper to taste

• • •

finely grated cheese, to serve

• • •

PREPARATION AND COOKING TIME: 40 MINUTES

This summery pasta dish is a delicious combination of courgettes and soft pasta bows flavoured with garlic and basil. Serve it with a choice of salads (pages 125–128).

Cook the pasta bows in plenty of boiling water for about 10 minutes, or until they are cooked through but still firm (*al dente*). Drain.

Meanwhile, heat the oil in a saucepan, add the courgettes, and sauté over a very gentle heat for about 5 minutes, or until they begin to soften. Then add the mushrooms, increase the heat a little and toss them in the oil until they too begin to soften. Lower the heat and stir in the garlic and basil. Cook very gently for a few minutes, stirring gently to mix, and then season to taste with salt and pepper. Mix with the pasta bows, toss thoroughly, and serve at once on hot plates, with grated cheese to sprinkle over the top.

PICTURED ON TITLE PAGE

TAGLIATELLE WITH CHINESE VEGETABLES

SERVES 4 AS A STARTER; OR 2 AS A MAIN COURSE

250 g (8 oz) tagliatelle

• • •

3 tablespoons sesame oil

• • •

6 spring onions, sliced

• • •

2.5 cm (1-inch) piece of root ginger, peeled and grated

• • •

125 g (4 oz) baby sweetcorn, sliced

• • •

125 g (4 oz) water chestnuts, cut into thin strips

• • •

125 g (4 oz) button mushrooms, quartered

• • •

125 g (4 oz) mange tout, sliced diagonally

• • •

2 tablespoons black bean or yellow bean sauce

• • •

2 tablespoons soy sauce

• • •

PREPARATION AND COOKING TIME: 20 MINUTES

The wonderful thing about pasta is its versatility. It lends itself to improvisation with herbs and spices of all kinds, sauces of all descriptions, and stuffings both simple and ornate. It is superb with these typical Chinese vegetables, lightly seasoned with ginger and soy sauce, and makes a supper dish with a difference.

Cook the tagliatelle in plenty of boiling water for about 10–12 minutes, or until it is cooked through but still firm (*al dente*).

Meanwhile, heat the oil in a saucepan, add the spring onions and ginger, and stir-fry for 2–3 minutes until they soften. Toss in all the remaining vegetables and stir-fry for about 4–5 minutes until they heat through and begin to soften. Then stir in the black bean or yellow bean sauce and soy sauce and heat through again, stirring all the time. Drain the tagliatelle and place it in a warm serving dish; pour over the vegetable mixture and toss thoroughly. Serve immediately.

BUCKWHEAT SPAGHETTI WITH TOMATOES AND SUMMER HERBS

SERVES 4

375 g (12 oz) buckwheat or wholewheat spaghetti

• • •

3 tablespoons olive oil

• • •

2 medium-size onions, sliced finely

• • •

1 large garlic clove, crushed

• • •

3 tablespoons mixed herbs, such as rosemary, tarragon, parsley lovage and thyme, chopped finely

• • •

397 g (14 oz) can of chopped tomatoes, drained, and juice reserved

• • •

salt and pepper to taste

• • •

finely grated cheese, to serve

• • •

PREPARATION AND COOKING TIME: 35 MINUTES

Buckwheat is gluten-free and spaghetti made from buckwheat flour has a stronger flavour than normal pasta. This simple recipe is one of my most faithful stand-bys – wonderful family food made in no time at all and always delicious. It is a summer dish, using fresh herbs when they are at their best in early summer and served with a tossed salad of chinese leaves, iceberg lettuce and watercress.

Cook the spaghetti in plenty of boiling water for about 10–12 minutes, or until it is cooked through but still firm (*al dente*).

Meanwhile, heat the oil in a large pan, add the onions and cook gently, stirring constantly for about 6–7 minutes or until they are softened but not browned. Stir in the garlic and herbs and cook for a further 5 minutes. Add the juice from the tomatoes and simmer for another 5 minutes. Add the tomatoes to the pan, season to taste with salt and pepper and heat through. Drain the spaghetti and transfer it to warm plates, covered with the sauce. Serve at once, with grated cheese to sprinkle over the top.

Tagliatelle with Chinese vegetables
Buckwheat spaghetti with tomatoes and summer herbs
Tagliatelle rosemarino
Pasta with broccoli and blue cheese

PASTA SHELLS WITH BLACK BEAN SAUCE

SERVES 4

300 g (10 oz) pasta shells

• • •

5 cm (2-inch) piece of root ginger, peeled and grated

• • •

2 tablespoons black bean sauce

• • •

2 tablespoons soy sauce

• • •

2 tablespoons hoisin sauce

• • •

175 ml (6 fl oz) vegetable stock

• • •

2 garlic cloves, crushed

• • •

grated zest of ½ lemon

• • •

3 tablespoons sesame oil

• • •

175 g (6 oz) button mushrooms, quartered

• • •

125 g (4 oz) bean sprouts

• • •

PREPARATION AND COOKING TIME: 15 MINUTES

*B*lack bean sauce is well worth buying as it gives a flavour quite out of the ordinary to any dish you add it to. This dish of pasta shells mixed with mushrooms and bean sprouts is seasoned with garlic and Chinese sauces, and it always seems to disappear as quickly as it is prepared.

Cook the pasta shells in plenty of boiling water for about 10 minutes, or until they are cooked through but still firm (*al dente*).

Meanwhile, mix together in a small saucepan the ginger, black bean sauce, soy sauce, hoisin sauce, stock, garlic and lemon zest. Allow the flavours to infuse over a very gentle heat for 5 minutes. Meanwhile, heat the sesame oil, add the mushrooms, and stir-fry until well coated in the oil. When the mushrooms are heated through but still crisp, add the bean sprouts, increase the heat and stir-fry briskly, so that they too heat through but are still crisp. Pour the sauce over the vegetables and mix together thoroughly. Drain the pasta and transfer it to warm plates, covered with the sauce. Serve immediately.

FETTUCCINE WITH MUSHROOMS AND CREAM

SERVES 4

375 g (12 oz) fettuccine

• • •

3 tablespoons olive oil

• • •

1 large onion, sliced finely

• • •

1 tablespoon dried mixed herbs

• • •

250 g (8 oz) mushrooms, sliced

• • •

142 ml (¼ pint) carton of single cream

• • •

2 eggs, beaten

• • •

salt and pepper to taste

• • •

finely grated cheese, to serve

• • •

PREPARATION AND COOKING TIME: 25 MINUTES

I cannot count the number of times I have cooked this classic pasta dish – and nobody has yet tired of it! Lovely soft textures and delicate tastes combine to provide a satisfying, nourishing meal that is quickly made, and needs only a tossed mixed salad of radicchio and feuille de chêne lettuce to go with it.

Cook the fettuccine in plenty of boiling water for about 10–12 minutes, or until it is cooked through but still firm (*al dente*).

Meanwhile, heat the oil in a saucepan, add the onion and sauté gently until thoroughly softened. Then stir in the herbs and cook for 1–2 minutes, stirring all the time. Add the mushrooms, stirring constantly until their juices start to run and they are softened. Stir the cream into the mixture and heat through.

Drain the fettuccine and transfer it to another saucepan. Cover with the sauce and put the pan over a very gentle heat. Stir in the eggs and cook slowly, stirring, until they begin to set lightly, rather like scrambled eggs. Season to taste with salt and pepper, and serve at once on warm plates. Hand a bowl of grated cheese around to sprinkle over the top.

Pasta shells with black bean sauce
Linguine with spicy sauce
Goat cheese and courgette lasagne with tomato coulis
Penne with basil

LINGUINE WITH SPICY SAUCE

SERVES 4

375 g (12 oz) linguine or spaghetti

* * *

4 tablespoons sunflower oil

* * *

2 garlic cloves, crushed

* * *

1–2 teaspoons garam masala paste

* * *

2 teaspoons ground turmeric

* * *

250 g (8 oz) chinese leaves, shredded finely

* * *

150 ml (¼ pint) vegetable stock

* * *

5 tablespoons soured cream or crème fraîche

* * *

salt to taste

* * *

PREPARATION AND COOKING TIME: 25 MINUTES

*P*ersonally I love spicy food, and I enjoy the heat and zest of chilli and garlic. So if you are like-minded, you will relish this combination of soft, bland pasta with a mixture of typically Indian spices. It is good served with warm naan bread and a side vegetable such as Creamy Broccoli Purée (page 79)

Cook the linguine or spaghetti in plenty of boiling water for 10–12 minutes, or until it is cooked through but still firm (*al dente*).

Meanwhile, heat the oil gently in a medium-size saucepan, add the garlic, garam masala and turmeric, and fry for a few minutes. Then add the chinese leaves and stir-fry until they are softened. Add the stock, heat through and season to taste with salt. Stir in the cream and mix well. When the sauce is smooth and even, drain the pasta, transfer it to warm plates and cover with the sauce, mixing thoroughly. Serve at once.

PASTA SALAD SPECIAL

SERVES 6

175 g (6 oz) small courgettes, sliced thinly

* * *

175 g (6 oz) celeriac, peeled and grated

* * *

1 yellow pepper, de-seeded and diced

* * *

125 g (4 oz) mange tout, sliced diagonally

* * *

125 g (4 oz) french beans

* * *

250 g (8 oz) pasta quills

* * *

2 tablespoons chopped dill

* * *

2 large garlic cloves, crushed

* * *

150 ml (¼ pint) olive oil

* * *

juice of 1 lemon

* * *

salt and pepper to taste

* * *

PREPARATION TIME: 20–30 MINUTES + 3 HOURS STANDING

*P*asta salads are wonderfully versatile: they are great to experiment with since there are so many exciting combinations to try. You can go for texture, colour, taste and aroma – and this recipe has them all in abundance.

Lightly steam the vegetables over boiling water until tender but firm. Cut into short lengths.

Meanwhile, cook the pasta quills in plenty of boiling water for about 10–12 minutes, or until they are cooked through but still firm (*al dente*). Drain.

Mix all the vegetables together in a bowl with the dill. Stir the garlic into the olive oil and toss the pasta quills in it. Then add the vegetables and lemon juice and mix well. Season to taste with salt and pepper. Leave the salad in a cool place for several hours before serving, tossing from time to time.

VEGETARIAN LASAGNE

> **SERVES 6**

4 tablespoons vegetable oil

• • •

375 g (12 oz) mushrooms, sliced

• • •

2 × 397 g (14 oz) can of chopped tomatoes, drained

• • •

250 g (8 oz) no-pre-cook lasagne sheets

• • •

432 g (14 oz) can of kidney beans, drained

• • •

400 g (13 oz) frozen spinach, defrosted and drained

• • •

450 ml (¾ pint) Béchamel Sauce (page 158)

• • •

75 g (3 oz) vegetarian Cheddar cheese, grated

• • •

2 eggs, beaten

• • •

salt, pepper and dried mixed herbs to taste

• • •

PREPARATION TIME: 20 MINUTES + 1 HOUR COOKING

*O*ne of the joys of this lasagne is that it is so easy to make, and can be prepared well in advance. All it needs to go with it is a tossed salad of frisée and Little Gem lettuces and some sliced yellow peppers.

Heat the oil in a large saucepan, add the mushrooms, and sauté briskly for about 5 minutes, or until they are lightly cooked and crisp. Set aside.

Cover the base of a large ovenproof dish with a layer of the tomatoes, and season to taste with salt, pepper and a sprinkling of the herbs. Cover with lasagne sheets, followed by a layer of kidney beans. Season again. Repeat, using a layer of lasagne followed first by the spinach and then by the mushrooms. Finish with a layer of lasagne.

Preheat the oven to Gas Mark 5/190°C/375°F. Heat the béchamel sauce gently, add the cheese and stir until it melts. Remove from the heat and stir in the beaten eggs. Pour this mixture over the top of the lasagne, and bake for 1 hour.

PASTA WITH BROCCOLI AND BLUE CHEESE

> **SERVES 6**

500 g (1 lb) pasta twists or shells

• • •

375 g (12 oz) broccoli, cut into small florets

• • •

142 ml (¼ pint) carton of single cream

• • •

125 g (4 oz) Danish blue cheese, crumbled finely

• • •

2 tablespoons chopped chives

• • •

pepper to taste

• • •

PREPARATION AND COOKING TIME: 20–25 MINUTES

A distinctive dish with strong flavours, this is ideal for cold winter weather when you want warming food. Serve it with a tossed salad of frisée and cos lettuces, accompanied by Sesame Pitta Bread (page 117).

Cook the pasta in plenty of boiling water for about 10–12 minutes, or until it is cooked through but still firm (*al dente*), adding the broccoli florets for the last 4–5 minutes of cooking. Drain thoroughly; then add the cream. Stir in the cheese and chives, and season to taste with salt and pepper. Serve immediately.

FOLLOWING PAGE (CLOCKWISE)
Toasted poppy-seed egg noodles
Fettuccine with mushrooms and cream
Pasta salad special
Spaghetti alla Genovese
Vegetarian lasagne
Courgettes with Chinese noodles and satay sauce

GOAT CHEESE AND COURGETTE LASAGNE WITH TOMATO COULIS

SERVES 6

FOR THE TOMATO COULIS
* * *
2 tablespoons olive oil
* * *
1 small onion, chopped finely
* * *
2 teaspoons plain flour
* * *
1 kg (2 lb) ripe tomatoes, skinned and chopped, or 2 × 397 g (14 oz) can of chopped tomatoes
* * *
a small bunch of herbs, chopped finely
* * *
2.5 cm (1-inch) piece of orange zest
* * *
salt to taste
* * *
FOR THE LASAGNE
* * *
1 kg (2 lb) small courgettes, sliced
* * *
a large bunch of basil, chopped
* * *
250 g (8 oz) soft goat cheese
* * *
250 g (8 oz) no-pre-cook lasagne sheets
* * *
300 ml (½ pint) Béchamel Sauce (page 158)
* * *
142 ml (¼ pint) carton of single cream
* * *
50 g (2 oz) vegetarian Cheddar cheese, grated
* * *
3 egg yolks
* * *
salt and pepper to taste
* * *
PREPARATION TIME: 1 HOUR + 1 HOUR COOKING

I make this wonderful lasagne when the tomato crop is at its height, and courgettes and basil are at their best. It is a stunning main course served with feuille de chêne lettuce and lollo rosso.

Heat the oil in a saucepan, add the onion, and fry gently, stirring, for 10 minutes. Stir in the flour and cook gently for a further 3 minutes. Stir in the remaining coulis ingredients; cover the pan and simmer for 5 minutes. Then remove the lid and simmer for a further 20 minutes, stirring occasionally. Add more water as necessary to prevent the mixture from sticking (but the final sauce should be quite thick).

Lightly steam the courgettes over boiling water for about 5–7 minutes, or until cooked through.

Moisten the bottom of a large ovenproof dish with a little tomato coulis. Cover with a layer of courgettes, season to taste with salt and pepper, and sprinkle with some basil. Cover with slices of goat cheese and moisten with a little more of the tomato coulis. Cover with sheets of lasagne. Repeat these layers, ending with a layer of lasagne.

Preheat the oven to Gas Mark 4/180°C/350°F.

Heat the béchamel sauce gently and stir in the cream. Add the Cheddar cheese and stir constantly until it melts, and then season to taste with salt and pepper. Remove the pan from the heat and beat in the egg yolks. Cover the top of the lasagne with this sauce and bake for 1 hour.

SPAGHETTI ALLA GENOVESE

SERVES 6

375 g (12 oz) tiny new potatoes, scrubbed and halved
* * *
250 g (8 oz) french beans, cut into 1 cm (½-inch) lengths
* * *
375 g (12 oz) wholewheat spaghetti
* * *
3 tablespoons olive oil
* * *
4 tablespoons pesto
* * *
chopped parsley, to garnish
* * *
finely grated cheese, to serve
* * *
PREPARATION TIME: 20 MINUTES + 20 MINUTES COOKING

This spaghetti dish uses an unusual combination of tiny new potatoes and french beans in season. The background flavour is of pesto, the now world-famous sauce from Genoa.

Boil the new potatoes for 3–4 minutes, then add the beans to the water and cook for a further 4–5 minutes. Drain and keep hot.

Meanwhile, in a separate pan, cook the spaghetti in plenty of boiling water for about 10–12 minutes, or until it is cooked through but still firm (*al dente*). Drain thoroughly, and toss it in the oil and the pesto, then add the potatoes and beans and mix well. Garnish with the chopped parsley and serve immediately, with grated cheese to pass around.

COURGETTES WITH CHINESE NOODLES AND SATAY SAUCE

SERVES 4

875 g (1¾ lb) courgettes, cut into 1 cm (½-inch) slices
* * *
4 tablespoons sesame oil
* * *
175 g (6 oz) oyster mushrooms, sliced
* * *
250 g (8 oz) Chinese egg noodles, soaked in boiling water
* * *
25 g (1 oz) dry-roasted peanuts, chopped
* * *
4–6 tablespoons Satay Sauce (page 152)
* * *
salt, pepper and soy sauce to taste
* * *
chopped coriander, to serve
* * *
PREPARATION TIME: 15–20 MINUTES

This is a delightfully different way of using courgettes, which lend themselves well to an oriental touch. You can make your own Satay Sauce (page 152) if you like.

Cut the courgette slices into quarters, blanch them in boiling water for 1–2 minutes and then drain. Heat a little of the oil in a saucepan, add the mushrooms, and sauté until lightly cooked. Drain the softened egg noodles, rinse them in cold water, and then shake them dry. Heat the remaining oil in a large pan or wok and add the noodles. When the noodles are heated through, add the vegetables, peanuts and satay sauce. Stir thoroughly until well mixed together, season to taste with salt, pepper and soy sauce and serve sprinkled with coriander.

TOASTED POPPY-SEED AND EGG NOODLES

SERVES 4

300 g (10 oz) Chinese egg noodles
* * *
1 egg, beaten
* * *
2 tablespoons milk
* * *
40 g (1½ oz) sunflower seeds
* * *
25 g (1 oz) poppy seeds
* * *
3 tablespoons sesame oil, plus extra for frying
* * *
25 g (1 oz) butter or margarine
* * *
4 spring onions, sliced very finely
* * *
salt and pepper to taste
* * *
PREPARATION AND COOKING TIME: 30 MINUTES

The crunch of toasted poppy seeds makes a mouth-watering contrast to soft egg noodles in this very simple dish, which is garnished with slivers of egg roll. It makes a tasty alternative to fried rice for a Chinese-style meal.

Cook the egg noodles in plenty of boiling water until they are cooked through but still firm (*al dente*).

Meanwhile, make the egg roll. Beat the egg with the milk and season to taste with salt and pepper. In a large pan, heat a small amount of oil and pour all of the egg mixture in. Fry for 2–3 minutes and then remove the thin egg roll from the pan. Roll it up tightly when it is cool, cut it into thin slices and set aside.

To toast the sunflower seeds, toss them in a heavy saucepan over moderate heat, with no added oil, until they are brown and crisp all over, shaking them frequently and taking care not to let them burn. Next, toast the poppy seeds by putting them in a tray under a medium grill and shaking them frequently until they are browned all over. Cool both the sunflower seeds and poppy seeds on kitchen paper.

Drain the noodles thoroughly and toss them in the sesame oil and butter or margarine. Add the sunflower seeds and spring onions and mix well. Turn the noodles into a warm serving dish, garnish with the sliced egg roll and sprinkle the toasted poppy seeds over the noodles. Serve at once.

PENNE WITH BASIL

SERVES 4

500 g (1 lb) penne
· · ·
6 tablespoons olive oil
· · ·
175 g (6 oz) button mushrooms, quartered
· · ·
2 garlic cloves, crushed
· · ·
3 tablespoons chopped basil
· · ·
142 ml (¼ pint) carton of single cream
· · ·
25 g (1 oz) pine kernels
· · ·
salt and pepper to taste
· · ·
basil leaves, to garnish
· · ·
PREPARATION TIME: 30 MINUTES

I would eat this every day throughout the basil season if I didn't have a little bit of respect for my waistline! Basil, garlic, pine kernels and cream are the dressing for this pasta dish, which is a perfect meal all on its own, followed perhaps by a fresh green salad of cos and Little Gem lettuces.

Cook the penne in plenty of boiling water for about 10–12 minutes, or until cooked through but still firm (*al dente*). Drain.

Heat the oil in a saucepan, add the mushrooms, and cook very rapidly for 3–4 minutes until they are slightly browned. Stir into the pasta with all the juices from the pan. Add the garlic and basil and stir in thoroughly; add the cream and heat through. Season to taste with salt and pepper, and finally stir in the pine kernels. Garnish each helping with basil leaves, and serve immediately.

TAGLIATELLE ROSEMARINO

SERVES 4

500 g (1 lb) fresh tagliatelle verdi
· · ·
50 g (2 oz) butter or margarine
· · ·
4 tablespoons finely chopped rosemary or
2 tablespoons dried rosemary
· · ·
142 ml (¼ pint) carton of single cream
· · ·
salt and pepper to taste
· · ·
grated parmesan or vegetarian Cheddar cheese, to serve
· · ·
PREPARATION TIME: 20 MINUTES

Rosemary's name derives from ros marinus, *dew of the sea, after its misty blue flowers: a fittingly beautiful name for one of the most aromatic of Mediterranean herbs. Rosemary dries very successfully, but I love to use it fresh when possible, early in the summer when the leaves are still young and tender.*

Cook the pasta in plenty of boiling water for about 3 minutes, or until it is cooked through but still firm (*al dente*).

Meanwhile, melt the butter or margarine in a large pan, add the chopped rosemary, and simmer for about 10 minutes or until it softens a little. Drain the pasta thoroughly and toss it in the rosemary butter. Pour in the cream, mix well and heat through. Season to taste with salt and pepper and serve with a sprinkling of cheese on each helping.

CHAPTER EIGHT

PULSES, GRAINS AND RICE

VEGETABLE FRIED RICE

SERVES 3–4

5 tablespoons vegetable oil
. . .
6 spring onions, sliced
. . .
2.5 cm (1-inch) piece of root ginger, peeled and grated
. . .
2 medium-size carrots, diced
. . .
1 medium-size pepper, de-seeded and diced
. . .
125 g (4 oz) frozen peas, defrosted
. . .
75 g (3 oz) bean sprouts
. . .
3 medium-size tomatoes, skinned and chopped
. . .
2 eggs, beaten
. . .
500 g (1 lb) cooked basmati rice
. . .
1–2 tablespoons soy sauce
. . .
1 tablespoon sesame oil
. . .

PREPARATION AND COOKING TIME: 25 MINUTES

There are innumerable variations on this theme, using seasonable vegetables. It makes a wonderful supper dish in its own right, served with a simple salad of chinese leaves and sliced radishes – or as part of a Chinese meal with a variety of other dishes.

Heat 4 tablespoons of the oil in a wok, add the spring onions, ginger and carrots, and stir-fry for 1 minute. Add the pepper, peas, bean sprouts and tomatoes, and stir-fry for another minute. Push all the vegetables to one side of the wok, and add the remaining oil to the pan. When it is hot, pour in the eggs and scramble them lightly. Add the rice to the vegetable side of the wok, and mix the egg thoroughly with the vegetables and rice. Stir and turn all the ingredients until evenly mixed. Season to taste with soy sauce and sesame oil, and serve as soon as possible.

BEST RISOTTO

SERVES 6

4 tablespoons vegetable oil

* * *

1 large onion, chopped finely

* * *

300 g (10 oz) long-grain rice, washed and drained

* * *

1 tablespoon dried mixed herbs

* * *

100 g (3½ oz) shelled peanuts

* * *

600 ml (1 pint) vegetable stock

* * *

175 g (6 oz) french beans, steamed and cut into short lengths

* * *

175 g (6 oz) mushrooms, sliced

* * *

125 g (4 oz) cooked peas

* * *

50 g (2 oz) vegetarian Cheddar cheese, grated

* * *

salt, pepper and ground mace to taste

* * *

chopped parsley, to garnish

* * *

finely grated cheese, to serve

* * *

PREPARATION TIME: 15 MINUTES + 30 MINUTES COOKING

My favourite memories of risotto are of improvisations, created by using whatever vegetables are around in the kitchen at the time. The resulting dish has character and originality, a kind of sparkle which does justice to risotto's Italian origins. You might like to add polenta (coarse corn meal) which is a common feature of northern Italian cuisine.

Heat the oil in a large saucepan, add the onion, and sauté for 5 minutes. Stir in the rice and mix until well coated with the oil. Add the herbs and peanuts and mix well. Then add the stock, a little at a time, simmering and stirring between each addition until the rice absorbs all the liquid.

Meanwhile, lightly steam the beans over boiling water for about 10 minutes, or until they are cooked but still crisp. When the rice has absorbed all the liquid, add the vegetables and cook gently, stirring, until they are hot and cooked through. Season to taste with salt, pepper and mace and stir in the cheese. When it has melted, serve the risotto on hot plates sprinkled with chopped parsley. Serve with grated cheese to sprinkle over the top.

VEGETABLE PAELLA

SERVES 6

25 g (1 oz) butter or margarine

* * *

1 large Spanish onion, chopped

* * *

2 tablespoons sunflower oil

* * *

375 g (12 oz) basmati rice

* * *

750 ml (1¼ pints) vegetable stock

* * *

6–8 saffron strands, soaked in a little stock

* * *

4 garlic cloves, chopped

* * *

175 g (6 oz) frozen peas, defrosted

* * *

350 g (11 oz) can of pimientos, chopped

* * *

175 g (6 oz) button mushrooms, quartered

* * *

4 large tomatoes, skinned and chopped

* * *

400 g (13 oz) can artichoke hearts, drained and halved

* * *

175 g (6 oz) mange tout, halved

* * *

227 g (8 oz) can whole water chestnuts, drained and sliced

* * *

salt and pepper to taste

* * *

finely grated cheese, to serve

* * *

PREPARATION TIME: 30 MINUTES + 35–40 MINUTES COOKING

Paella makes an eye-catching and mouth-watering meal. Here I substitute mushrooms, artichoke hearts, mange tout and water chestnuts for the traditional fish. Serve it with a tossed salad of watercress, sliced fennel and feuille de chêne lettuce.

Melt the butter or margarine in a large frying-pan or wok, add the onion, and cook slowly over a gentle heat for about 10 minutes until soft and transparent. Add the rice and cook for 3–4 minutes over a medium heat, stirring constantly. Add the stock, a little at a time, simmering between each addition until it is absorbed. After about 10 minutes, add the saffron and garlic and continue cooking for 5 minutes, or until the rice is fully cooked. Then stir in all the remaining ingredients and cook over a gentle heat, stirring occasionally, for about 10 minutes, or until heated through. Check the seasoning. Serve as soon as possible, with grated cheese.

PICTURED ON PAGE 10

SOFT VEGETABLE RICE CHINESE-STYLE

SERVES 4–6

3 tablespoons vegetable oil

• • •

375 g (12 oz) broccoli, cut into small florets and stalk chopped

• • •

4 medium-size carrots, sliced

• • •

300 ml (½ pint) vegetable stock

• • •

300 g (10 oz) basmati rice, cooked

• • •

2 teaspoons Chinese 5-spice powder

• • •

1 teaspoon ground ginger

• • •

soy sauce to taste

• • •

2 hard-boiled eggs, chopped

• • •

6 spring onions, sliced finely

• • •

PREPARATION TIME: 20 MINUTES + 35 MINUTES COOKING

*T*his version of rice with vegetables is very well-cooked and – as its title suggests – soft. The vegetables become almost inseparable from the rice, and the dish is then seasoned with soy sauce and Chinese 5-spice powder. Comforting, nourishing food which I like to serve on cold winter evenings.

Heat the oil in a 1.5-litre (2½-pint) flameproof casserole dish. Add the broccoli and carrots and stir-fry for 2–3 minutes. Add the stock and stir in the rice until it is well mixed with the vegetables. Cover the casserole and simmer over a very low heat, for 25 minutes, stirring occasionally to ensure that the rice does not stick to the pan. When the vegetables are almost integrated with the rice, season to taste with 5-spice, ginger and soy sauce. Add half the eggs and half the spring onions. Stir until heated through and well-mixed; check the seasoning. Serve hot, garnished with the remaining hard-boiled egg and spring onions.

LENTIL AND MUSHROOM SLICE

SERVES 4

175 g (6 oz) green lentils, soaked for 1 hour

• • •

1 bay leaf

• • •

1 large onion, chopped finely

• • •

175 g (6 oz) button mushrooms, halved and sliced

• • •

25 g (1 oz) butter or margarine, plus extra for greasing

• • •

1 tablespoon chopped parsley

• • •

6 tablespoons vegetable stock

• • •

1 egg, beaten

• • •

75 g (3 oz) vegetarian Cheddar cheese, grated

• • •

1 tablespoon dried mixed herbs

• • •

salt and pepper to taste

• • •

PREPARATION TIME: 10 MINUTES + 1 HOUR SOAKING
+ 45–50 MINUTES COOKING + 5–10 MINUTES STANDING

*T*his simple dish is in great demand by my family – they love its wholesome tastes and its satisfying texture. It freezes well, and makes a perfect meal served with steamed side vegetables, a tossed salad of radicchio and iceberg lettuce and warm Sage Bread (page 122).

Drain the soaked lentils and cover them with cold water. Bring to the boil with the bay leaf and simmer for about 25–30 minutes or until tender.

Preheat the oven to Gas Mark 5/190°C/375°F. Drain the lentils, remove the bay leaf and mix with all the remaining ingredients. Season to taste with salt and pepper. Grease a 1.5-litre (2½-pint) loaf tin, cover the base with the mixture and bake for 45–50 minutes, or until set. Leave the savoury loaf to rest in the tin for at least 5–10 minutes before you turn it out. Serve hot, warm or cold.

FOLLOWING PAGE (CLOCKWISE)
Vegetable fried rice
Spinach dhal
Saffron rice with pine kernels and cheese
Sushi rice with cumin
Best risotto
Soft vegetable rice Chinese-style
Sauce poivre-vert (PAGE 152)

SPICY CHICK-PEA CASSEROLE

SERVES 6

250 g (8 oz) dried chick-peas, soaked overnight, or
432 g (15 oz) can chick-peas, drained

· · ·

500 g (1 lb) spinach, stalks removed

· · ·

1½ tablespoons sunflower oil

· · ·

2 onions, sliced

· · ·

2 garlic cloves, sliced

· · ·

2 teaspoons ground cumin

· · ·

2 teaspoons ground coriander

· · ·

2 teaspoons garam masala powder

· · ·

1 teaspoon ground ginger

· · ·

1 bay leaf

· · ·

175 g (6 oz) courgettes, diced

· · ·

75 g (3 oz) raisins

· · ·

salt and soy sauce to taste

· · ·

PREPARATION AND COOKING TIME: 1 HOUR 20 MINUTES + SOAKING OVERNIGHT

This spicy casserole is very flavoursome, and the addition of raisins makes it quite distinctive. It is delicious hot, warm or cold, served with buttered noodles.

Drain and rinse the dried chick-peas, cover with fresh water, bring to the boil and simmer for 40–50 minutes, or until tender. Drain and set aside, reserving the cooking liquid.

Lightly cook the spinach in boiling water for about 5 minutes. Drain well, and then squeeze out any excess moisture before chopping it. Heat the oil in a large saucepan, add the onions and garlic, and cook gently, stirring occasionally, for 10 minutes. Add the spices and bay leaf and cook, stirring occasionally, for a further 5 minutes. Add 600 ml (1 pint) of the reserved cooking liquid or water to the casserole, bring to the boil and simmer for a minute or two. Add the chick-peas, spinach, courgettes and raisins, and a little more water if necessary. Simmer for 10 minutes. Remove the bay leaf and season to taste with salt and soy sauce. Serve as soon as possible.

BUTTERBEAN AND LEEK GRATIN

SERVES 4–6

250 g (8 oz) dried butterbeans, soaked overnight, or
2 × 220 g (7 oz) can butterbeans, drained

· · ·

3 medium-size leeks, chopped

· · ·

½ cauliflower, separated into florets

· · ·

25 g (1 oz) butter or margarine

· · ·

1 small onion, chopped

· · ·

2 garlic cloves, chopped

· · ·

1 tablespoon plain flour

· · ·

1 teaspoon ground coriander

· · ·

250 ml (8 fl oz) vegetable stock

· · ·

1–2 tablespoons coarse-grain mustard

· · ·

1 teaspoon clear honey

· · ·

5 tablespoons single cream (optional)

· · ·

50 g (2 oz) vegetarian Cheddar cheese, grated finely

· · ·

125 g (4 oz) fresh breadcrumbs

· · ·

salt and pepper to taste

· · ·

PREPARATION TIME: 55–65 MINUTES + SOAKING OVERNIGHT + 30 MINUTES COOKING

A hearty dish in which a mixture of butterbeans, leeks and cauliflower is spiced with coriander and topped with a cheesy breadcrumb topping.

Drain and rinse the dried butterbeans and then cover with water. Simmer for 45–50 minutes until tender; then drain, reserving the cooking liquid.

Meanwhile, cook the leeks and cauliflower in boiling water for about 15 minutes. Drain well and set aside. Melt the fat, add the onion and garlic and cook for 5–8 minutes or until soft. Sprinkle over the flour and stir for a further 5 minutes. Add the coriander and season to taste; then add the stock and bean cooking liquid, stirring constantly until smooth. Stir in the mustard and honey and cook over a low heat.

Preheat the oven to Gas Mark 4/180°C/350°F. Combine the beans with the leeks and cauliflower, and stir in the sauce and cream, if used. Season to taste. Put into an ovenproof dish. Mix the cheese and breadcrumbs together, sprinkle over the top and bake for 30 minutes.

SHEPHERDESS PIE

> SERVES 6–8

250 g (8 oz) aduki beans, soaked overnight

• • •

1 bay leaf

• • •

1 tablespoon soy sauce

• • •

500 g (1 lb) potatoes, peeled

• • •

500 g (1 lb) leeks, sliced

• • •

2 teaspoons dried sage

• • •

3–4 tablespoons sunflower oil

• • •

1 large onion, diced

• • •

1 small carrot, grated

• • •

1 celery stick, sliced finely

• • •

50 g (2 oz) mushrooms, sliced

• • •

1 tablespoon chopped basil

• • •

1 teaspoon dried rosemary

• • •

½ teaspoon mustard powder

• • •

50 g (2 oz) plain flour

• • •

2 tablespoons milk

• • •

25 g (1 oz) butter or margarine

• • •

a pinch of nutmeg

• • •

50 g (2 oz) vegetarian Cheddar cheese, grated

• • •

salt, pepper and soy sauce to taste

• • •

PREPARATION TIME: 1¼ HOURS + SOAKING OVERNIGHT + 30 MINUTES COOKING

A vegetarian version of shepherd's pie, this is nourishing family food that is a meal in itself, and needs only a light green salad of chinese leaves, cos lettuce and sliced baby courgettes to accompany it.

Drain and rinse the beans, cover with fresh water, add the bay leaf and boil for 30–40 minutes until quite tender. Drain and remove the bay leaf; then add the soy sauce. Boil the potatoes for about 20 minutes, or until quite soft. Drain, reserving the liquid.

Steam the leeks over boiling water with the sage for about 10 minutes, or until tender. Heat the oil in a large saucepan, add the onion, and fry for 5 minutes. Add the carrot and celery and stir-fry for 2 minutes. Then add the mushrooms and basil and continue cooking for another 3–4 minutes, or until the mushrooms are just tender. Season to taste with salt and pepper, or soy sauce. Add the rosemary and mustard. Sprinkle in the flour and stir well. Stir in enough of the potato cooking water to make a thin sauce and simmer, stirring constantly, for 5 minutes. Check the seasoning.

Mix the aduki beans with the leeks and stir them into the sauce. Place the mixture in a deep ovenproof casserole dish.

Preheat the oven to Gas Mark 4/180°/350°F. Mash the potatoes with the milk and butter or margarine, and season with salt, pepper and the nutmeg. Smooth over the vegetables and spread the cheese on top. Bake for 30 minutes.

BULGAR WHEAT WITH SPINACH AND GARLIC

> SERVES 4

375 g (12 oz) spinach

• • •

4 tablespoons vegetable oil

• • •

2 garlic cloves, crushed

• • •

1 large onion, sliced finely

• • •

175 g (6 oz) bulgar wheat, soaked in hot water for 20 minutes until the grains swell

• • •

300 ml (½ pint) vegetable stock

• • •

salt and pepper to taste

• • •

PREPARATION TIME: 5–10 MINUTES + 20 MINUTES SOAKING + ABOUT 15 MINUTES COOKING

Quick and simple to prepare, this combination of bulgar wheat with spinach and garlic makes a warming meal, ideal for homely suppers on winter evenings. It is delicious served with a simple tomato salad and warm french bread or Sesame Pitta Bread (page 117).

Lightly cook the spinach in boiling water for about 5 minutes; drain and squeeze out any excess water before chopping it.

Heat the oil in a large frying-pan or saucepan, add the garlic and onion, and sauté for 3–4 minutes or until softened. Drain the bulgar wheat, add it to the pan and stir until well mixed. Add the stock and spinach and stir well. Simmer for 10 minutes, stirring occasionally, and then season to taste with salt and pepper. Serve hot or warm.

FLAGEOLETS WITH CAULIFLOWER AND GARLIC

SERVES 4

3 tablespoons sunflower oil

· · ·

1 spanish onion, sliced finely

· · ·

2 garlic cloves, crushed

· · ·

½ medium-size cauliflower, separated into small florets

· · ·

2 teaspoons ground coriander

· · ·

432 g (14 oz) can flageolet beans, drained

· · ·

4 tablespoons chopped coriander leaves

· · ·

salt to taste

· · ·

PREPARATION TIME: 5 MINUTES + 15 MINUTES COOKING

This is a great favourite of mine: a warming dish of cauliflower and flageolet beans spiced with coriander and garlic. Serve it with plain buttered rice and a crunchy side salad of chinese leaves and iceberg or cos lettuce.

Heat the oil in a large frying-pan, add the onion and garlic, and sauté over a gentle heat until they turn transparent and soft. Increase the heat a little and add the cauliflower to the mixture, stirring until well coated in the oil. Lower the heat and add the ground coriander; then cover the pan and cook for 5–6 minutes. Add the beans, increase the heat again and stir the mixture until the beans are heated through. Add 3 tablespoons of the chopped coriander, and season to taste with salt. Continue cooking for a further 2–3 minutes, and then turn into a serving dish, sprinkle with the remaining coriander and serve.

Butterbean and leek gratin
Shepherdess pie
Tomato and orange sauce (PAGE 155)
Lentil and mushroom slice

SPINACH DHAL

SERVES 4–6

250 g (8 oz) green lentils, soaked for 1 hour

· · ·

½ teaspoon ground turmeric

· · ·

2 large garlic cloves, crushed

· · ·

1 large onion, chopped

· · ·

1 bay leaf

· · ·

5 cm (2-inch) piece of root ginger, peeled and bruised

· · ·

500 g (1 lb) cooked spinach

· · ·

230 g (7 oz) can of chopped tomatoes, drained

· · ·

2 teaspoons ground cumin

· · ·

2 teaspoons ground coriander

· · ·

2 tablespoons olive oil

· · ·

1 teaspoon cumin seeds, crushed

· · ·

¼ teaspoon mustard seeds, crushed

· · ·

salt to taste

· · ·

PREPARATION AND COOKING TIME: 50 MINUTES + 1 HOUR SOAKING

This spinach dhal makes a wonderfully satisfying meal served with buttered rice or noodles and a crisp side salad of lollo rosso, feuille de chêne lettuce and sliced radishes.

Drain and rinse the soaked lentils. Put them in a saucepan with the turmeric, garlic, onion, bay leaf and ginger, and cover with water. Bring to the boil, cover the pan and simmer for 25–30 minutes, or until the lentils are completely soft. Stir in the tomatoes and spinach. Add the spices, and leave to cook over a very gentle heat for 10 minutes, stirring from time to time and adding more water if necessary. Season to taste with salt, remove the bay leaf and transfer the mixture to a serving dish. Just before serving, heat the olive oil in a small pan and fry the cumin and mustard seeds until the latter begin to pop. Pour over the dhal and serve.

KIBBEH

SERVES 6

1 small cauliflower, divided into small florets
• • •
250 g (8 oz) millet
• • •
900 ml (1½ pints) water
• • •
2 small onions, chopped
• • •
2 teaspoons ground cumin
• • •
1 teaspoon garam masala powder
• • •
2–3 tablespoons sunflower oil
• • •
2 garlic cloves, crushed
• • •
1 carrot, cut into strips
• • •
1 green pepper, de-seeded and sliced finely
• • •
175 g (6 oz) mushrooms, sliced
• • •
1 large aubergine, diced
• • •
2 teaspoons chopped coriander leaves
• • •
1 teaspoon ground ginger
• • •
1 teaspoon ground coriander
• • •
2 tablespoons sunflower seeds
• • •
salt, pepper and soy sauce to taste
• • •

PREPARATION TIME: 40–50 MINUTES + 25–30 MINUTES COOKING

A recipe from the Middle East, where millet is popular. This is a gently spiced dish in which a layer of sautéed vegetables is covered with a mouth-watering layer of millet cooked with cauliflower. The topping of sunflower seeds gives it a delectable crunch.

Put the cauliflower and millet into a saucepan with the water and simmer for about 20 minutes or until all the water is absorbed. Stir in half the onions, the cumin and garam masala, and season to taste with salt and pepper.

Heat 1 tablespoon oil, add the remaining onions and the garlic, and sauté for 5–10 minutes until soft. Add the carrot and pepper and stir-fry until they begin to soften. Add the remaining oil, and stir in the mushrooms and aubergine. Cover, and cook until the aubergine has softened. Stir occasionally to prevent the mixture from sticking, and add a little water if necessary.

Preheat the oven to Gas Mark 4/180°C/350°F. Add the coriander and spices, and season to taste with soy sauce.

Check the seasoning, and pour into a large ovenproof dish. Cover with the millet and cauliflower mixture, and sprinkle the sunflower seeds on top. Bake for 25–30 minutes until browned.

MILLET PILAV

SERVES 4

4 tablespoons vegetable oil
• • •
250 g (8 oz) millet, washed and drained
• • •
1 garlic clove, crushed
• • •
600 ml (1 pint) vegetable stock
• • •
1 large onion, sliced
• • •
1 teaspoon garam masala powder
• • •
½ teaspoon ground turmeric
• • •
50 g (2 oz) pine kernels or flaked almonds, toasted
• • •
salt to taste
• • •
chopped parsley, to garnish
• • •
natural yogurt, to serve
• • •

PREPARATION TIME: 30 MINUTES + 30–35 MINUTES COOKING

This simple pilav consists of millet cooked with sautéed onion and garlic, with some browned pine kernels thrown in for added texture and flavour. It makes a satisfying supper dish, and is delicious with Red and White Salad with Watercress (page 128).

Heat half the oil in a heavy-bottomed saucepan, add the millet and stir over a moderate heat for about 15 minutes, or until it begins to brown. Add the garlic, stock, and a little salt to taste, and then bring to the boil. Cover the pan and simmer for about 15–20 minutes, or until all the water is absorbed. Remove from the heat and leave to stand in the pan for 10 minutes to finish softening.

Heat the remaining oil in a saucepan, add the onion, garam masala and turmeric and sauté for about 15–20 minutes, or until the onion is golden. Stir this into the millet with the pine kernels or almonds. Garnish with parsley and serve with natural yogurt to pass around.

Spicy chick-pea casserole
Sauce cressonnière (PAGE 154)
Flageolets with cauliflower and garlic
Millet pilav

KASHA WITH GARLIC MUSHROOMS

SERVES 4

sunflower oil for frying

• • •

175 g (6 oz) roasted buckwheat

• • •

450 ml (¾ pint) water

• • •

75 g (3 oz) butter or margarine

• • •

375 g (12 oz) flat mushrooms, sliced

• • •

2 large garlic cloves, crushed

• • •

salt to taste

• • •

PREPARATION AND COOKING TIME: 25 MINUTES

My Russian friend introduced me to this way of cooking buckwheat, and I immediately took to it. The aroma of roasted buckwheat as it cooks is incredibly appetising, and the combination with garlicky mushrooms makes a wholesome meal.

Heat the oil in a saucepan, add the buckwheat and toss it in the oil until it pops. Add the water and a little salt, and bring to the boil. Simmer, partially covered, for 10–12 minutes, stirring occasionally, until the buckwheat has absorbed all the water and is quite tender. Remove from the heat, and leave to cool a little.

Meanwhile, melt 50 g (2 oz) of the butter or margarine in a saucepan, add the mushrooms, and sauté for about 5 minutes, or until they begin to soften. Then stir in the garlic, and cook gently for a further 2–3 minutes until all the juices have run and the garlic is well mixed.

Add the remaining butter or margarine to the buckwheat and stir it in thoroughly. Heap the mixture into a serving dish and surround with the garlic mushrooms. Serve at once.

SAFFRON RICE WITH PINE KERNELS AND CHEESE

SERVES 6

50 g (2 oz) butter or margarine

• • •

250 g (8 oz) basmati rice, washed

• • •

4 cardamom pods, crushed

• • •

50 g (2 oz) sugar, dissolved in 600 ml (1 pint) warm water

• • •

½ teaspoon saffron strands, soaked in a little water

• • •

50 g (2 oz) pine kernels, toasted

• • •

25 g (1 oz) parmesan or vegetarian Cheddar cheese, grated

• • •

25 g (1 oz) finely chopped pistachio nuts, to garnish

• • •

PREPARATION AND COOKING TIME: 30 MINUTES

The inspiration for this recipe comes from Persia. Middle Eastern cuisine makes good use of saffron, and traditionally for special feasts they highlight its beautiful golden colour by decorating the dishes with gold leaf. Serve it with Japanese Five-colour Salad (page 125).

Melt the butter or margarine in a large saucepan, over a gentle heat. Add the rice and stir for about 2 minutes. Add the cardamom pods and sweetened water, which should amply cover the rice. Add the soaked saffron, stir well and bring to the boil. Cover the pan and simmer gently for 10 minutes, or until the rice is almost tender. Add the pine kernels and cheese, and cook for a further 5 minutes until the rice is completely cooked through and tender. Remove the pan from the heat and allow it to stand, covered, for 2–3 minutes. Then fluff up the rice, and serve it sprinkled with the pistachios.

Bulgar wheat with spinach and garlic
Kasha with garlic mushrooms
Couscous
Kibbeh

COUSCOUS

SERVES 6

500 g (1 lb) couscous

* * *

4 tablespoons sunflower oil

* * *

3 garlic cloves, crushed

* * *

2 medium-size onions, quartered

* * *

6 small courgettes, diced

* * *

2 medium-size yellow peppers, de-seeded and sliced

* * *

6 small new potatoes, scrubbed and chopped

* * *

4 medium-size carrots, sliced lengthways

* * *

2 small turnips, peeled and sliced

* * *

100 g (3½ oz) chick-peas, cooked and drained

* * *

397 g (14 oz) can of chopped tomatoes, drained

* * *

125 g (4 oz) raisins or sultanas, soaked in warm water for 10 minutes and drained

* * *

2 teaspoons ground coriander

* * *

2 teaspoons ground cumin

* * *

1 teaspoon ground turmeric

* * *

salt to taste

* * *

PREPARATION TIME: 30 MINUTES + 50 MINUTES COOKING

Although this Arab dish takes time to prepare, it is worth the effort. Serve it with Granary bread or Thyme Oatcakes (page 124).

Put the couscous in a large bowl and stir in 600 ml (1 pint) water. Drain immediately and stand for 15 minutes, turning from time to time to prevent them becoming lumpy.

Heat the oil in a large saucepan, add the garlic, onions, courgettes, peppers, potatoes, carrots and turnips, and chick-peas; then sauté them over a moderate heat, stirring constantly, for 10 minutes. Add 600 ml (1 pint) water and bring to the boil. Put the couscous into a sieve and stand it, covered with a lid, over the vegetables. Simmer for 30 minutes.

Remove the couscous and set aside. Stir the tomatoes and raisins or sultanas into the vegetables, add the spices and season with salt. Replace the couscous above the vegetables and simmer for 10 minutes, stirring constantly. Drain off some of the liquid, transfer to a large serving dish, and cover with the vegetables. Serve at once.

SUSHI RICE WITH CUMIN

SERVES 8

125 ml (4 fl oz) white wine vinegar

* * *

175 g (6 oz) sugar

* * *

1 tablespoon salt

* * *

1½ tablespoons ground cumin

* * *

500 g (1 lb) long-grain rice, washed and drained

* * *

900 ml (1½ pints) water

* * *

toasted sesame seeds, to garnish

* * *

PREPARATION TIME: 25 MINUTES + 12 MINUTES COOKING

These little square patties of rice are an original addition to a buffet table or a smörgåsbord. Spicing with cumin turns ordinarily bland rice into mouth-watering morsels. They go particularly well with a cucumber salad.

Mix the vinegar, sugar, salt and cumin in a saucepan and bring to the boil, stirring until well mixed. Remove from the heat and set the dressing aside.

Place the rice and water in a saucepan and bring the water to the boil. Stir the rice, lower the heat and simmer very gently, covered, for 10–12 minutes, or until all the water is absorbed. Be sure not to lift the lid while the rice is cooking: the steam is essential for cooking it. Fluff the rice, and pour the dressing over it, mixing it in thoroughly. Leave it to cool slightly for 10 minutes.

While it is still warm, shape tablespoons of the mixture into square patties on a rinsed chopping board. The patties are traditionally served just warm or cold, but they can be reheated by steaming. Sprinkle the patties with the toasted sesame seeds.

CHAPTER NINE

PASTRIES, PIES AND BREADS

CHEESY COURGETTE STRUDEL

SERVES 4–6

25 g (1 oz) butter or margarine, melted, plus extra for greasing

• • •

3 tablespoons olive oil

• • •

8 fillo pastry sheets 30 × 15 cm (12 × 6 inches)

• • •

500 g (1 lb) courgettes, steamed and sliced

• • •

125 g (4 oz) mange tout, steamed and sliced diagonally

• • •

175 g (6 oz) Gruyère or goat cheese, grated finely

• • •

1 egg, beaten

• • •

salt and pepper to taste

• • •

PREPARATION TIME: 15–20 MINUTES + 30–40 MINUTES COOKING
+ 5 MINUTES STANDING

This sensational pastry roll encases lightly cooked courgettes and mange tout which are bound together with melted cheese. It is delightfully simple to prepare, and naturally you can experiment by varying the vegetables. Serve it with boiled new potatoes and a fresh herb salad.

Mix the melted butter or margarine with the olive oil. Brush 4 of the sheets of fillo pastry with this mixture, placing them one on top of another, and keeping the remaining sheets covered with a damp tea towel or clingfilm, to prevent drying and cracking.

Mix together the vegetables and cheese. Season to taste with salt and pepper. Take half the mixture and spread it over the surface of the pastry, allowing an 8 cm (3-inch) margin at both ends, and a 5 cm (2-inch) margin along the sides. Fold the ends inwards, and then lift the side margins over to cover the filling and form the strudel into a long roulade shape.

Preheat the oven to Gas Mark 5/190°C/375°F. Place the strudel on a well-greased baking sheet and brush the surface with beaten egg. Repeat with the remaining half of the ingredients. Bake for 30–40 minutes, until golden-brown. Allow the strudels to stand for 5 minutes or so before you slice them. Serve on a warmed serving dish.

CRUSTY PIZZA

MAKES TWO 23CM (9-INCH) PIZZAS

FOR THE BASE

· · ·

1 quantity Basic Wholemeal Bread dough (page 121)

· · ·

flour for rolling

· · ·

FOR THE FILLING

· · ·

2 tablespoons olive oil

· · ·

1 medium-size onion, chopped finely

· · ·

1 garlic clove, crushed

· · ·

125 g (4 oz) mushrooms, sliced

· · ·

397 g (14 oz) can of tomatoes, drained, reserving juice

· · ·

2 teaspoons dried mixed herbs

· · ·

1 small courgette, sliced thinly

· · ·

½ green or yellow pepper, de-seeded and sliced finely

· · ·

½ teaspoon chilli powder (Cayenne)

· · ·

salt and pepper to taste

· · ·

FOR THE TOPPING

· · ·

125 g (4 oz) mozzarella cheese, sliced

· · ·

1 green pepper, de-seeded and sliced

· · ·

12 black olives

· · ·

PREPARATION TIME: 25 MINUTES + 20–25 MINUTES COOKING

There is nothing quite like a home-made pizza, made with your own fresh bread dough for the base. The smells from the kitchen are mouth-watering, and these pizzas make an unbeatable meal, served with a crisp side salad of iceberg lettuce and watercress.

Take the risen dough and knead it lightly on a floured board. Divide into two, and roll into two rounds about 5 mm (¼ inch) thick. Lay the bases in 2 well-greased 23 cm (9-inch) cake tins so that the base and the sides are covered. Cover with a tea towel and put in a warm place to rise while you prepare the filling.

Heat the oil in a saucepan, add the onion and fry gently until soft, adding the garlic after about 5 minutes. Add the mushrooms and cook for a further 2 minutes, stirring. Drain the tomatoes, reserving the juice, and add them to the pan with the herbs, courgette and pepper, stir well and then simmer for 3–4 minutes. Add the juice from the tomatoes if necessary – the mixture should not be too dry. Season to taste with salt, pepper and chilli powder (Cayenne). Set aside to cool a little.

Preheat the oven to Gas Mark 6/200°C/400°F. Pour the cooled filling on to the risen pizza bases and top with the mozzarella, green pepper and olives. Bake for 20–25 minutes, or until the bases are cooked and the topping is golden-brown.

PUFF-PASTRY TRIANGLES

MAKES 6

375 g (12 oz) mixed vegetables of your choice, such as cauliflower, mushrooms, leeks, courgettes, broccoli, carrots, mange tout, fennel, peas, spinach – all chopped or sliced and cooked al dente

· · ·

300 ml (½ pint) Béchamel Sauce (page 158)

· · ·

25 g (1 oz) vegetarian Cheddar cheese, grated

· · ·

500 g (1 lb) puff pastry

· · ·

flour for rolling

· · ·

1 egg, beaten

· · ·

1 tablespoon sesame seeds

· · ·

salt and paprika to taste

· · ·

PREPARATION TIME: 15–20 MINUTES + 15 MINUTES COOKING

These puff-pastry triangles have become a regular stand-by with my family. I vary the fillings according to the time of year, choosing seasonal vegetables to ring the changes. Serve them with a tossed salad of radicchio and cos lettuce.

Stir the vegetables into the béchamel sauce and mix thoroughly. Stir in the cheese and leave the mixture to cool.

Preheat the oven to Gas Mark 7/220°C/425°F. Roll out the puff pastry fairly thinly and cut into six 13 cm (5-inch) squares. Moisten the edges with water. Place one-quarter of the mixture in the centre of each square, and season with salt and paprika to taste. Take one corner of the pastry and fold it over to the opposite corner. Press the edges of the triangle together with a fork, so that they are well sealed. Brush with the beaten egg and sprinkle with the sesame seeds. Place on a baking sheet, and bake for 12–15 minutes until the pastry is risen and golden.

YORKSHIRE PUDDING WITH STIR-FRIED VEGETABLES

> SERVES 6

FOR THE BATTER
* * *
1 egg
* * *
125 g (4 oz) plain flour, sifted
* * *
a pinch of salt
* * *
300 ml (½ pint) milk
* * *
3 tablespoons vegetable oil
* * *
FOR THE FILLING
* * *
3 tablespoons vegetable oil
* * *
500 g (1 lb) mixed vegetables of your choice, such as broccoli, cauliflower, mange tout, carrots, courgettes, peas, brussels sprouts, bean sprouts, mushrooms – all cut into thin strips as necessary
* * *
5 spring onions, chopped finely
* * *
soy sauce to taste
* * *

PREPARATION TIME: 20 MINUTES + 2 HOURS STANDING + 25 MINUTES COOKING

*F*illing a Yorkshire pudding with a stir-fry of vegetables of your choice makes an inspired meal that is lovely for Sunday dinner with roast potatoes and cauliflower cheese. You can also fill the Yorkshire pudding with creamed or puréed vegetables, and serve it with Chinese Carrot and Coriander Salad (page 130).

Beat the egg into the sifted flour and salt, and then gradually add the milk to make a smooth batter. (You can also do this using a food processor.) Leave the batter to stand for 2 hours.

Preheat the oven to Gas Mark 7/220°C/425°F). Put oil into a 25 cm (10-inch) round baking tin and place in the oven until it is hot. Pour in the batter and return to the oven for 25 minutes until well risen and golden.

Meanwhile, heat the oil in a large saucepan, add the vegetables, and stir-fry them with the spring onions for 4–5 minutes, or until cooked through but still crunchy. Season to taste with soy sauce.

When the Yorkshire pudding is cooked, remove it from the tin and fill with the vegetable mixture. Serve hot or warm.

LEEK PARCELS WITH GOAT CHEESE

> SERVES 4

500 g (1 lb) leeks, cooked and chopped
* * *
3 tablespoons double cream
* * *
15 g (½ oz) butter or margarine, plus extra for greasing
* * *
2 teaspoons dried green peppercorns, crushed
* * *
75 g (3 oz) goat cheese, mashed
* * *
500 g (1 lb) puff pastry
* * *
flour for rolling
* * *
1 egg, beaten
* * *
salt to taste
* * *

PREPARATION TIME: 20 MINUTES + 20 MINUTES COOKING

*T*he simple device of wrapping leeks in pastry parcels makes a spectacular dish. The combined flavours of goat cheese with green peppercorns are epicurean, and I love to surprise people with it. These are delicious served with new potatoes and a tossed mixed salad with Garlic Vinaigrette (page 133).

Mix the leeks with the cream. Heat the butter or margarine in a saucepan, add the peppercorns, and sauté gently for about 5 minutes. Stir these into the goat cheese and blend to a smooth mixture with the leeks. Season to taste with salt.

Preheat the oven to Gas Mark 6/200°C/400°F. Roll the pastry out thinly and cut it into four 18 cm (7-inch) squares. Place one quarter of the leek mixture in the centre of each square and moisten the edges with water. Fold over to form a rectangle, and press the edges together with a fork to seal them securely. Brush with the beaten egg and place on a baking sheet. Bake for 20 minutes, until the pastry is well risen and golden.

MUSHROOM AND WATERCRESS CHOUX PUFFS

SERVES 4–6

FOR THE CHOUX PASTE
· · ·
75 g (3 oz) butter or margarine, plus extra for greasing
· · ·
150 ml (¼ pint) water
· · ·
125 g (4 oz) plain flour, sifted
· · ·
4 eggs, beaten
· · ·
salt and pepper to taste
· · ·
1 tablespoon grated parmesan cheese or other hard cheese (optional)
· · ·
FOR THE FILLING
· · ·
50 g (2 oz) butter or margarine
· · ·
500 g (1 lb) mushrooms, chopped
· · ·
a bunch of watercress, chopped (reserve some whole sprigs, to garnish)
· · ·
150 ml (¼ pint) Béchamel Sauce (page 158)
· · ·
salt to taste
· · ·

PREPARATION AND COOKING TIME: ABOUT 1 HOUR + COOLING

The addition of watercress to a purée of mushrooms is inspired – together they make a tangy filling for these golden choux puffs. Serve with a vegetable such as Summer Squash 'Cockaigne' (page 80) and a salad of Little Gem and frisée lettuces with sliced yellow peppers.

To make the choux paste, put the butter or margarine and the water into a thick-bottomed saucepan and bring to the boil. When the fat has melted, briskly stir in the flour and seasonings, and stir thoroughly until the mixture is very smooth and glossy. Remove the pan from the heat and cool slightly; then gradually stir in the eggs, beating until they are absorbed and the mixture is smooth and shiny.

Preheat the oven to Gas Mark 6/200°C/400°F. Place the mixture in 12 large tablespoonfuls on 2 well-greased baking sheets, leaving some distance between the choux puffs since they swell considerably during cooking. Sprinkle with the cheese if used and bake for 20 minutes, or until the puffs are well risen and golden. Turn off the oven and leave the puffs there for 10 more minutes. Make a slit in each puff to allow steam to escape, and leave to cool on a wire rack.

Heat the butter or margarine in a large saucepan, add the mushrooms, and cook gently for about 10 minutes, or until soft. Add the watercress and stir over a moderate heat for 4–5 minutes or until soft. Liquidise to a purée with the béchamel sauce. Season to taste with salt. Use this mixture to fill the choux puffs. Garnish with the watercress sprigs and serve.

BEST LEEK PIE

SERVES 4–6

6 tablespoons vegetable oil, plus extra for greasing
· · ·
175 g (6 oz) plain flour, sifted
· · ·
salt
· · ·
1½ tablespoons cold water
· · ·
3 tablespoons sunflower oil
· · ·
500 g (1 lb) leeks, chopped
· · ·
2 garlic cloves, sliced
· · ·
2 eggs, beaten
· · ·
3 tablespoons milk
· · ·
175 g (6 oz) feta cheese, crumbled finely
· · ·

PREPARATION TIME: 45 MINUTES + 25–30 MINUTES COOKING

I love leeks – their fine flavour graces any dish whether simple or elaborate, and they are delicious in this pie, flavoured with a little garlic and mixed with feta cheese. It is lovely served with boiled new potatoes and a simple tomato salad.

Preheat the oven to Gas Mark 3/160°C/325°F. Stir the oil into the flour and salt and mix well; then add the water and knead to a dough. Press it with your knuckles into a well-oiled 20 cm (8-inch) flan tin. Bake for 10–15 minutes until lightly browned. Cool on a wire rack.

Turn the oven up to Gas Mark 5/190°C/375°F. Heat the oil in a saucepan, add the leeks and garlic, and cook gently for about 10 minutes, stirring constantly, until soft. Mix the eggs thoroughly with the milk. Stir in the cheese and fold in the leeks. Pour this filling into the prepared pastry case. Bake for 25 minutes until well browned. Serve hot, warm or cold.

VEGETABLE MILLE-FEUILLES

SERVES 4

500 g (1 lb) puff pastry

1 egg, beaten

125 g (4 oz) cooked peas

125 g (4 oz) cooked asparagus

50 g (2 oz) butter or margarine, plus extra for greasing

5 tablespoons Béchamel Sauce (page 158) or soured cream

a little single cream

750 g (1½ lb) mixed vegetables such as asparagus, mange tout, broccoli florets, peas, courgettes, sweetcorn, spinach

PREPARATION AND COOKING TIME: ABOUT 1 HOUR

It occurred to me once that mille-feuilles don't necessarily have to be the domain of sweet patisserie: so why not try savoury ones? I did – and these are the result. They are wonderful: elegant, appetising food which melts in the mouth.

Preheat the oven to Gas Mark 6/200°C/400°F. Roll the pastry out thinly and cut it into eight 13 × 5 cm (5 × 2-inch) rectangles. Brush each one with the beaten egg and place on a well-greased baking tray. Bake for about 15–20 minutes, or until well risen and golden. Split the pastry puffs lengthways about one-third of the way up their height, and keep hot.

To make the sauce, liquidise the cooked vegetables, butter or margarine, béchamel sauce or soured cream and cream to a very smooth purée. Thin out if necessary with a little more single cream.

To make the filling, cut the vegetables into short lengths or small cubes and steam them over boiling water for about 10 minutes, or until they are tender but still crisp. Mix with the sauce so they are lightly coated, and heat through. Pile the mixture on to the bottom layer of each mille-feuille and cover with the top layer of pastry. Serve immediately.

PICTURED ON PAGE 10

SESAME PITTA BREAD

MAKES 6 LARGE PITTAS

300 ml (10 fl oz) hot water

1 tablespoon dried yeast

1 tablespoon clear honey

50 g (2 oz) strong white flour, plus extra for rolling

2 tablespoons olive oil, plus extra for greasing

½ teaspoon salt

300 g (10 oz) plain wholemeal flour

125 g (4 oz) sesame seeds, toasted

PREPARATION TIME: 30 MINUTES + 1 HOUR 10 MINUTES RISING + 10–20 MINUTES COOKING

Pitta is a popular bread for all kinds of occasions, and this version, made with toasted sesame seeds, is especially tasty.

Put the water, yeast and honey into a large bowl and leave to stand for about 5 minutes, until the mixture is frothy.

Stir in the strong white flour, oil, salt, 125 g (4 oz) of the wholemeal flour, and the sesame seeds, and beat for 3 minutes. Then work in the rest of the wholemeal flour to make a pliable dough, adding more hot water if necessary. Turn it on to a well-floured board and knead for about 5–10 minutes. Place in a lightly oiled bowl and turn until completely covered with the oil. Cover, and leave to rise in a warm place for about 1 hour or until doubled in bulk.

Preheat the oven to Gas Mark 6/200°C/400°F. Knead the dough again and divide it into 6. Roll each on a floured board to make 20 cm (8-inch) diameter circles about 5 mm (¼ inch) thick. Place on well-oiled baking sheets and stand for 10 minutes. Bake for 4 minutes on each side until puffed. Remove from the oven and slit each one open along part of one side. Wrap in a clean tea towel until ready to serve.

PICTURED ON TITLE PAGE

FOLLOWING PAGE (CLOCKWISE)
Yorkshire pudding with stir-fried vegetables
Sauce Normande (PAGE 158)
Best leek pie
Cheesy courgette strudel
Mushroom brioches
Leek parcels with goat cheese
Mushroom and watercress choux puffs

MUSHROOM BRIOCHES

MAKES 6

7 g (¼ oz) dried yeast

. . .

2 tablespoons warm water

. . .

15 g (½ oz) caster sugar

. . .

125 g (4 oz) plain wholemeal flour, plus extra for rolling

. . .

125 g (4 oz) plain flour

. . .

1 teaspoon salt

. . .

150 g (5 oz) butter or margarine, plus extra for greasing

. . .

2 eggs, beaten

. . .

125 g (4 oz) button mushrooms, chopped

. . .

1 garlic clove, crushed

. . .

½ tablespoon thick-set natural yogurt

. . .

salt and pepper to taste

PREPARATION TIME: 50 MINUTES + 45 MINUTES RISING + 20 MINUTES COOKING

S oft, yeasty brioche dough is baked with a filling of cooked chopped mushrooms, and is quite irresistible. These are lovely with Creamy Broccoli Purée (page 79), or with Sauce Béarnaise (page 155) and a tossed salad of feuille de chêne lettuce and radicchio.

Dissolve the yeast in the warm water with 1 teaspoon of sugar. Allow it to stand in a warm place for 5 minutes until it becomes frothy.

Sift the flours with the remaining sugar, and the salt. Dice 125 g (4 oz) of the butter or margarine into the flour, and fold in the beaten eggs. Mix well, then stir in the dissolved yeast. The dough will be very sticky. With floured hands knead the dough for 3–4 minutes on a generously floured board, until smooth and light. Put it in a warm place, covered, while you prepare the filling.

Melt the remaining butter or margarine in a large pan, add the mushrooms, and cook gently, stirring until they soften and the juices begin to run. Add the garlic, and cook for a further 2 minutes. Season to taste with salt and pepper. Allow the filling to cool, and drain; then mix with the yogurt.

Preheat the oven to Gas Mark 6/200°C/400°F. Roll out the dough and cut into six circles 10 cm (4 inches) in diameter and 1 cm (½ inch) thick. Brush the edges with beaten egg.

Place 1–2 tablespoons of the mushroom mixture in the centre of each circle, gather up the edges, and then crimp them together. Place them on a well-greased baking sheet, cover and put in a warm place for 45 minutes until they have doubled in size. Bake for 20 minutes until the brioches are golden-brown and fully risen. Serve hot or warm.

CHAPATIS

MAKES 10–12

375 g (12 oz) wholemeal or plain flour, plus extra for rolling

. . .

1 teaspoon salt

. . .

250 ml (8 fl oz) water

. . .

oil for greasing

. . .

50 g (2 oz) butter, melted

. . .

PREPARATION TIME: 20 MINUTES + 1 HOUR STANDING + 50–60 MINUTES COOKING

H ome-made chapatis are very simple to prepare, and – as with all breads – they always seem so much tastier than any commercial variety. Delicious for a light lunch with Lebanese Hummus (page 27), or with any curry (pages 51–58).

Sift the flour with the salt. Gradually add enough water to make a soft, pliable dough. Cover and leave to stand for 1 hour.

Grease your hands with a little oil and knead the dough vigorously for 5 minutes. Divide it into 10–12 small ball shapes. Flatten them out one by one on a floured board, and roll out thinly to 18 cm (7-inch) circles.

Lightly grease a heavy frying-pan or griddle and heat until smoking; then cook the chapatis for about 2–3 minutes on each side, or until brown spots appear. Brush immediately with melted butter. Keep the chapatis wrapped in foil in a warm oven, until ready to serve.

PICTURED ON PAGE 52

BASIC WHOLEMEAL BREAD

MAKES 1 LARGE LOAF

25 g (1 oz) fresh yeast, or 15 g (1/2 oz) dried yeast

• • •

1 teaspoon sugar

• • •

350 ml (12 fl oz) warm water

• • •

375 g (12 oz) plain wholemeal flour, plus extra for rolling

• • •

250 g (8 oz) plain flour

• • •

1 teaspoon salt

• • •

2–3 tablespoons sunflower oil, plus extra for greasing

• • •

PREPARATION TIME: 20 MINUTES + 1 HOUR RISING + 35–40 MINUTES BAKING + COOLING

Making your own bread is one of the most satisfying experiences on earth. The wonderful fragrances of rising dough and of baking bread are followed by the incomparable experience of eating the loaf fresh and still warm from the oven when it is at its most irresistible.

If using dried yeast, follow the instructions on the packet; if using fresh yeast, mix it with the sugar and a little of the warm water, adding the rest of the water when the mixture is smooth. Set aside in a warm place until the mixture is frothy.

In a large mixing bowl, sift the flours with the salt and mix with the oil. Make a well in the centre and pour the yeast mixture into this. Flick some flour over the top and fold in with a wooden spoon, until the dough starts to become elastic. Then knead thoroughly on a floured board for 5 minutes, until light and smooth.

Put into a clean, oiled bowl and cover with a tea towel. Leave to rise in a warm place for 40 minutes. Knead the dough for a further 5 minutes; then form it into a loaf shape. Place in an oiled 1 kg (2 lb) loaf tin, make three diagonal incisions across the loaf and cover with a tea towel. Put in a warm place and leave to rise for 20 minutes.

Preheat the oven to Gas Mark 6/200°C/400°F and bake for 35–40 minutes, until well browned. Cool on a wire rack for a few minutes, then invert and turn out. Leave to cool.

PICTURED ON PAGE 26

INDIAN PURIS

MAKES 15

250 g (8 oz) plain wholemeal flour, plus extra for rolling

• • •

1 teaspoon salt

• • •

50 g (2 oz) butter or margarine

• • •

75–150 ml (3–5 fl oz) cold water

• • •

oil for deep-frying

• • •

PREPARATION AND COOKING TIME: 20 MINUTES + 1 HOUR STANDING

My favourite of all the Indian breads, these deep-fried puris are irresistible. Serve them with a curry (pages 51–58), or as an alluring contribution to a buffet table.

Sift the flour with the salt, and rub in the butter or margarine until the mixture resembles fine breadcrumbs. Stir in enough water to make a pliable dough. Knead on a lightly floured board until the dough is smooth and elastic. Cover with a cloth and leave in a warm place for 1 hour.

Roll out the dough on a lightly floured board until it is paper-thin. Cut into circles 10 cm (4 inches) in diameter. Cover them with a damp cloth as you cut, to prevent them drying out. Heat the oil in a deep-frying pan, and deep-fry the puris, one at a time, holding them gently under the surface of the oil until they puff and turn golden. Lift out with a slotted spoon, and drain on kitchen paper. Serve as soon as possible.

PICTURED ON PAGE 143

IRISH SODA BREAD

MAKES ONE 500 g (1 lb) LOAF

375 g (12 oz) plain white flour, plus extra for rolling

• • •

125 g (4 oz) plain wholemeal flour

• • •

2 teaspoons bicarbonate of soda

• • •

a pinch of salt

• • •

1 teaspoon sugar

• • •

2 tablespoons wheatgerm (optional)

• • •

284 ml (½ pint) carton of buttermilk

• • •

butter or margarine for greasing

• • •

PREPARATION TIME: 5 MINUTES + 30–35 MINUTES COOKING

My Irish friend Pauline gave me this recipe for the soda bread that she makes regularly for her family. It is delicious, and so quick and easy to make that it has become part of my repertoire too!

Preheat the oven to Gas Mark 6/200°C/400°F. Sift the flours with the soda, salt, sugar, and wheatgerm if used. Stir in enough buttermilk to make a wet dough, and knead a little on a floured board. Put into a well-greased 500 g (1 lb) loaf tin and bake for 30 minutes. Leave to cool on a wire rack for 5 minutes before turning the loaf out.

PICTURED ON PAGE 20

SAGE BREAD

MAKES ONE 500 g (1 lb) LOAF

25 g (1 oz) fresh yeast or 15 g (½ oz) dried yeast

• • •

1 teaspoon sugar

• • •

a little warm water

• • •

250 g (8 oz) self-raising flour

• • •

250 g (8 oz) plain wholemeal flour

• • •

1 teaspoon salt

• • •

2 tablespoons dried sage

• • •

25 g (1 oz) butter or margarine

• • •

300 ml (½ pint) milk

• • •

oil for greasing

• • •

PREPARATION TIME: 1½ HOURS + 2¼ HOURS RISING
+ 30 MINUTES BAKING + 10 MINUTES RESTING

It is extremely hard to resist this bread as it cools after baking, but spare some for the next day if you can: it makes scrumptious hot buttered toast.

Dissolve the yeast with the sugar and the water. Sift the flours with the salt and stir in the dried sage. Melt the butter or margarine and mix it with the milk. Make a well in the centre of the flour and pour in the yeast. Cover it with flour from around the edge and then pour in the milk and butter mixture. Mix to a soft dough and knead until smooth. Cover and leave to rise in a warm place such as an airing cupboard for 1–1½ hours. Then 'knock it back', by kneading thoroughly once more, and put it into a well-oiled 500 g (1 lb) loaf tin. Leave to rise for a further 45 minutes in a warm place.

Meanwhile, preheat the oven to Gas Mark 7/220°C/425°F. Bake the loaf for 15 minutes and then reduce the oven temperature to Gas Mark 5/190°C/375°F and bake for a further 15 minutes. Allow to rest for 10 minutes, and then turn the loaf out and cool it on a wire rack.

PICTURED ON PAGE 17

Minted cucumber flan
Puff-pastry triangles
Crusty pizza
Sauce Dijonnaise (PAGE 154)

THYME OATCAKES

MAKES 6

250 g (8 oz) porridge oats

• • •

1 tablespoon dried thyme

• • •

½ teaspoon bicarbonate of soda

• • •

1 teaspoon salt

• • •

25 g (1 oz) butter or margarine

• • •

1 egg yolk

• • •

oil for greasing

• • •

PREPARATION TIME: 10 MINUTES + 30 MINUTES BAKING

Oatcakes eaten with cheese are amongst the best of British food, and herb oatcakes are even better!

Preheat the oven to Gas Mark 4/180°C/350°F. Mix the oatmeal and thyme with the bicarbonate of soda and salt. Rub in the butter or margarine and stir in the egg yolk. Mix to a soft dough with a little hot water and knead until smooth. Press into a well-greased 20 cm (8-inch) flan tin and bake for 30 minutes. Mark into 6 triangles with a sharp knife, and allow to cool.

PICTURED ON PAGE 23

MINTED CUCUMBER FLAN

SERVES 4

125 g (4 oz) plain flour

• • •

½ teaspoon salt

• • •

50 g (2 oz) butter or margarine

• • •

2–3 tablespoons cold water

• • •

175 g (6 oz) curd cheese

• • •

4 tablespoons single cream or milk

• • •

3 sprigs of mint or 2 teaspoons dried mint

• • •

1 garlic clove, crushed

• • •

75 g (3 oz) vegetarian Cheddar cheese, grated finely

• • •

½ large cucumber, peeled and sliced thinly

• • •

3 eggs, beaten

• • •

salt and pepper to taste

• • •

PREPARATION TIME: 30 MINUTES + 20–25 MINUTES BAKING + CHILLING

The taste of mint is a powerful one, but when it is used in the right balance, with the right ingredients, I think it is unbeatable. It goes particularly well with this combination of soft cheese and cucumber, and the resulting flan is unusual and memorable.

Preheat the oven to Gas Mark 6/200°C/400°F. Sift the flour with the salt and rub in the butter or margarine until the mixture resembles breadcrumbs. Add the water and form the pastry into a ball. Press it, without kneading, into a greased 20 cm (8-inch) flan tin. Prick the pastry surface evenly with a fork and bake blind in the oven for 10 minutes. Lower the oven temperature to Gas Mark 4/180°C/350°F.

Mash the curd cheese with the cream or milk until smooth. Chop the mint leaves finely and stir in all but a few of them, with the garlic and 50 g (2 oz) of the Cheddar cheese. Season to taste with salt and pepper and fill the flan case with this mixture. Cover it with the slices of cucumber. Season the beaten eggs, mix in the rest of the mint, and pour this over the top. Sprinkle with the remaining Cheddar cheese and bake for 20–25 minutes until the eggs are set. Cool, and serve chilled.

CHAPTER TEN

SALADS AND RAW FOOD

JAPANESE FIVE-COLOUR SALAD

SERVES 4–6

FOR THE DRESSING
• • •
125 g (4 oz) tofu
• • •
2 tablespoons sesame seeds
• • •
2 teaspoons caster sugar
• • •
2 teaspoons cider vinegar
• • •
½ teaspoon salt
• • •
FOR THE SALAD
• • •
125 g (4 oz) mooli, peeled and cut into thin strips
• • •
1 medium-size carrot, peeled and sliced into very thin rounds
• • •
125 g (4 oz) green beans, trimmed
• • •
75 g (3 oz) button mushrooms, quartered
• • •
75 g (3 oz) dried apricots, chopped finely
• • •
strips of lemon zest, to garnish
• • •
PREPARATION AND COOKING TIME: 25 MINUTES + STANDING

An elegant mixture of five different colours, this salad is dressed with an oriental dressing based on tofu, or soya bean curd.

Mash the tofu in a bowl. Toast the sesame seeds until golden-brown; then cool them a little, and crush them to a paste in a mortar. Stir the paste into the tofu. Stir in the sugar, vinegar and salt until the dressing is smooth.

Steam the mooli and carrot for 2 minutes; then rinse them under cold water immediately. Steam the beans for 3 minutes and repeat the cooling process. Combine the vegetables with the mushrooms and apricots, and stir into the white dressing. Toss well. Leave to stand for 1–2 hours to allow the flavours to develop, and then serve garnished with the strips of lemon zest.

NUT-BUTTER CAULIFLOWER SALAD

SERVES 4-6

FOR THE DRESSING
· · ·
2 tablespoons crunchy peanut butter
· · ·
2 tablespoons grapeseed or olive oil
· · ·
1 tablespoon raspberry vinegar
· · ·
salt to taste
· · ·
FOR THE SALAD
· · ·
1 medium-size cauliflower
· · ·
½ fresh pineapple, skinned
· · ·
1 red apple, cored and sliced
· · ·
1 banana, sliced
· · ·
8–10 seedless grapes, halved
· · ·
tarragon sprigs, to garnish
· · ·
PREPARATION TIME: 15–20 MINUTES

A crunchy sauce, made with peanut butter, makes an unusual dressing for this mixture of cauliflower and fresh fruits. A delicious starter, and a popular addition to a buffet table.

Mix the peanut butter thoroughly with the oil, and gradually stir in the vinegar. Season to taste with salt.

Cut the cauliflower into small, bite-size florets. Cut the pineapple into small cubes. Mix all the salad ingredients together and toss immediately in the dressing. Pile into a salad bowl or on to a plate lined with the leaves from the cauliflower. Garnish with sprigs of tarragon.

SPICY BULGAR WHEAT SALAD

SERVES 6-8

175 g (6 oz) bulgar wheat
· · ·
2 teaspoons garam masala powder
· · ·
1 teaspoon ground turmeric
· · ·
1 teaspoon paprika
· · ·
175 g (6 oz) brussels sprouts, trimmed and sliced thinly
· · ·
2 oranges, peeled, segmented and chopped
· · ·
198 g (7 oz) can of sweetcorn, drained
· · ·
75 g (3 oz) dry-roasted peanuts
· · ·
1 tablespoon grapeseed or olive oil
· · ·
PREPARATION TIME: 15–20 MINUTES + 20–30 MINUTES STANDING

B ulgar wheat makes a satisfying base for a mixed salad. It makes a delicious meal served with Aubergine Salad (page 129), and Creamy Butterbean Dip with Herbs (page 25).

Put the bulgar wheat into a large bowl and pour boiling water over it to cover. Leave to stand for 15 minutes, until it has absorbed the water and is quite soft. Fold in all the remaining ingredients, and leave for 20–30 minutes so that the flavours can develop before serving.

*Leek and tomato salad with saffron
Salade de fenouil avec tomates
Nut-butter cauliflower salad
Salad Bagration*

RED AND WHITE SALAD WITH WATERCRESS

SERVES 4

FOR THE DRESSING
* * *
juice of 1 lemon
* * *
1 tablespoon clear honey
* * *
3 tablespoons grapeseed or olive oil
* * *
½ teaspoon salt
* * *
FOR THE SALAD
* * *
¼ small red cabbage
* * *
¼ small white cabbage
* * *
a bunch of watercress
* * *
25 g (1 oz) sesame seeds, toasted
* * *
PREPARATION TIME: 15 MINUTES

Lines of red and white cabbage, surrounded by a ring of watercress, make an eye-catching salad of excellent texture and flavour. A lemony dressing gives it a sharp tang.

Whisk all the dressing ingredients together until smooth.

Shred both cabbages very finely indeed. Arrange the watercress around the edge of a large, flat salad dish. Lay lines of alternating red and white cabbage across the dish, and sprinkle with the sesame seeds. Spoon the dressing over the top and serve.

CHICORY AND SWEET PEPPER SALAD WITH CORIANDER

SERVES 6

2 yellow peppers, de-seeded and quartered
* * *
3 heads of chicory, sliced finely
* * *
125 g (4 oz) bean sprouts
* * *
a small bunch of coriander, chopped
* * *
5 tablespoons Garlic Vinaigrette (page 133)
* * *
50 g (2 oz) flaked almonds, toasted
* * *
PREPARATION TIME: 30 MINUTES

Grilling peppers has the effect of sweetening their flavour considerably as well as softening them. They make a delectable contrast to crisp chicory and bean sprouts, and the addition of fresh coriander gives the salad its distinctive flavour.

Grill the peppers, skin-side up, until the skin blisters. Leave to cool; then peel and slice them. Mix the peppers with the chicory, bean sprouts and coriander and put into a salad bowl. Dress with the garlic vinaigrette and toss well. Sprinkle the almonds over the top of the salad just before serving.

PICTURED ON PAGE 11

SALADE DE FENOUIL AVEC TOMATES

SERVES 4

250 g (8 oz) fennel, trimmed

* * *

125 g (4 oz) tomatoes

* * *

juice of 1 lemon

* * *

salt to taste

* * *

finely chopped parsley, to garnish

* * *

PREPARATION TIME: 10 MINUTES

This recipe comes from a French friend who is a superb cook and runs an elegant table. Like so many simple French dishes, it is nevertheless memorable.

Slice the fennel and cut it into small pieces. Slice the tomatoes thinly. Mix together with the lemon juice and season with a little salt. Put into a dish and garnish with chopped parsley.

LEEK AND TOMATO SALAD WITH SAFFRON

SERVES 2

250 g (8 oz) small leeks, trimmed

* * *

450 ml (³/4 pint) vegetable stock

* * *

1 teaspoon dried thyme

* * *

3–4 saffron strands

* * *

1 bay leaf

* * *

150 g (5 oz) tomatoes, skinned, halved and de-seeded

* * *

salt and pepper to taste

* * *

TO GARNISH

* * *

1 hard-boiled egg, chopped

* * *

chopped parsley

* * *

PREPARATION TIME: 15 MINUTES + 30 MINUTES COOKING + OVERNIGHT CHILLING

Inspired by a classic French dish, this is a salad of chilled cooked vegetables, with the aromas of bay, saffron and thyme to enrich them. It makes a lovely light lunch dish, served with Wholemeal Bread (page 121) or Granary rolls.

Place the leeks in a saucepan with the stock and add the thyme, saffron and bay leaf. Cover the pan and simmer very gently for 20 minutes. Add the tomatoes, season to taste with salt and pepper, and simmer for a further 10 minutes. Drain, leaving enough of the liquid to just cover the vegetables. Cool, and chill overnight.

Remove the bay leaf and arrange the vegetables decoratively in a dish. Pour the juices over the top. Serve garnished with the egg and parsley.

AUBERGINE SALAD

SERVES 4–6

500 g (1 lb) aubergines

* * *

2–3 garlic cloves, crushed

* * *

3 tablespoons finely chopped parsley

* * *

¹/2 teaspoon dried thyme

* * *

olive oil

* * *

375 g (12 oz) tomatoes, skinned and sliced

* * *

salt and pepper to taste

* * *

chopped coriander, to garnish

* * *

PREPARATION TIME: 15 MINUTES + 20–25 MINUTES COOKING + COOLING

Lines of sliced, skinned tomatoes are overlapped with a garlicky, aromatic purée of cooked aubergine, and the dish is garnished with chopped coriander. Serve it with Sesame Pitta Bread (page 117) to make a delectable meal.

Preheat the oven to Gas Mark 4/180°C/350°F. Bake the aubergines for 20–25 minutes, until completely soft. Cool; then scoop out the flesh. Blend it with the garlic to a smooth purée. Add the herbs, and stir in enough oil to bring to a spreading consistency. Season to taste with salt and pepper.

Arrange a line of sliced tomatoes along a serving plate. Partially cover with some of the aubergine purée. Arrange another line of tomato slices overlapping, and continue until all the ingredients have been used. Sprinkle with chopped coriander just before serving.

SALAD BAGRATION

SERVES 4

FOR THE DRESSING

• • •

300 ml (½ pint) Mayonnaise (page 158)

• • •

2 medium-size tomatoes, skinned and chopped very finely

• • •

salt and pepper to taste

• • •

FOR THE SALAD

• • •

75 g (3 oz) macaroni

• • •

2 artichoke hearts, diced

• • •

150 g (5 oz) celeriac, peeled and cut into thin strips

• • •

2 hard-boiled eggs, sliced

• • •

chopped parsley, to garnish

PREPARATION TIME: 25 MINUTES

This recipe comes from an old French collection I borrowed from a friend. It was the dressing, a mixture of chopped tomatoes with mayonnaise, that drew my attention, and when I tried it out using this combination of artichoke hearts, macaroni and celeriac I was quite bowled over. An excellent meal in itself, served with a tossed salad of chinese leaves, iceberg lettuce and sliced radishes, together with french bread or oatcakes.

Mix the mayonnaise with the tomatoes. Season to taste with salt and pepper.

Cook the macaroni in plenty of boiling water for 10–12 minutes until it is cooked through but still firm (*al dente*). Drain and leave to cool.

Mix the artichoke hearts with the macaroni and celeriac, and toss well. Mix with two-thirds of the tomato mayonnaise. Check the seasoning, pour into a shallow serving dish and pipe the remaining mayonnaise on the top. Edge with the eggs, and sprinkle a little chopped parsley over the top.

CHINESE CARROT AND CORIANDER SALAD

SERVES 4

FOR THE DRESSING

• • •

1 tablespoon black bean sauce

• • •

1 tablespoon raspberry vinegar

• • •

1 tablespoon soy sauce

• • •

1 tablespoon grated ginger

• • •

4 tablespoons sesame oil

• • •

FOR THE SALAD

• • •

375 g (12 oz) carrots, grated finely

• • •

a large bunch of coriander, chopped

• • •

PREPARATION TIME: 10 MINUTES

I make this salad throughout the year and it never fails to delight. It is simple to make, and its Chinese flavours are fabulous.

Whisk together all the dressing ingredients.

Mix the carrots with the coriander and toss in the Chinese dressing, until thoroughly mixed. Transfer the salad to a serving dish.

Japanese five-colour salad
Indonesian salad
Red and white salad with watercress
Chinese carrot and coriander salad

INDONESIAN SALAD

SERVES 4–6

FOR THE SALAD

• • •

1 medium-size potato

• • •

175 g (6 oz) broccoli, cut into florets

• • •

125 g (4 oz) french beans

• • •

½ cucumber, cut into thin strips

• • •

2 medium-size carrots, cut into thin strips

• • •

4–5 chinese leaves, shredded

• • •

3 hard-boiled eggs, quartered

FOR THE DRESSING

• • •

25 g (1 oz) desiccated coconut

• • •

300 ml (½ pint) boiling water

FOR THE SAUCE

• • •

2.5 cm (1-inch) piece of root ginger, peeled and grated

• • •

2 garlic cloves, chopped

• • •

1 fresh chilli, de-seeded and chopped

• • •

2 spring onions, chopped

• • •

3 tablespoons sunflower oil

• • •

175 g (6 oz) dry-roasted peanuts, ground coarsely

• • •

2 teaspoons sugar

• • •

juice of 1 lemon

• • •

salt to taste

• • •

PREPARATION AND COOKING TIME: 25 MINUTES + 3 HOURS STANDING

A salad of lightly cooked vegetables, dressed in a characteristically Indonesian dressing. Ginger, garlic and chilli are the predominant flavours, ground peanuts the predominant texture, and the dressing is moistened with coconut 'milk'. It makes a wonderful addition to a buffet table, or an excellent simple meal in its own right, served with Indian Puris (page 121).

Cook the potato in boiling water for about 15 minutes, or until tender; drain and leave to cool. Cut the potato into small cubes.

Meanwhile, steam the broccoli florets and french beans over boiling water for 3–4 minutes, until they are tender but still crisp. Leave to cool, and then cut the french beans into 1 cm (½-inch) lengths. Mix with all the remaining vegetables and the eggs, and put into a serving dish.

Pour the boiling water over the coconut and leave to stand for 10 minutes or so, and then drain and reserve the coconut milk.

Put the ginger, garlic, chilli and spring onions into a small bowl and blend to a paste. Heat the oil in a saucepan, add the paste and fry for 2–3 minutes. Add all the remaining sauce ingredients, including the coconut milk. Simmer until the sauce thickens.

Dress the prepared vegetables with the sauce, mix well, and leave for a few hours at room temperature before serving.

GREEN LETTUCE ROLLS

SERVES 4

2 round lettuces, washed

• • •

1 cucumber, peeled

• • •

125 g (4 oz) ripe Brie, rind removed

• • •

150 g (5 oz) mange tout, trimmed

• • •

1 tablespoon chopped basil or dill

• • •

250 g (8 oz) cottage cheese

• • •

salt and pepper to taste

PREPARATION TIME: 20 MINUTES + CHILLING

These delectable rolls are filled with soft cottage cheese mixed with cucumber, mange tout and Brie. The subtle flavour of basil or dill highlights the filling, and the rolls are as appetising as they look.

Select the larger, outer leaves of the lettuce and use the hearts for a tossed green salad. Remove the hard central stalk from each outer lettuce leaf. Cut the cucumber and Brie into tiny dice, and slice the mange tout diagonally, very finely. Combine these with the herbs. Blend the cottage cheese smoothly to a purée. Mix all the vegetables into the cottage cheese and season to taste with salt and pepper. Place a spoonful of the filling in the centre of each lettuce leaf and roll it up, tucking in the ends to make a parcel. Chill until ready to serve.

VINAIGRETTE

> **MAKES 175 ML (6 FL OZ)**

2 tablespoons lemon juice or tarragon vinegar
* * *
2 teaspoons mild French mustard
* * *
150 ml (1/4 pint) olive oil
* * *
salt and pepper to taste
* * *
1 garlic clove, crushed (optional), for Garlic Vinaigrette
* * *
PREPARATION TIME: 5–10 MINUTES

Mix the lemon juice or vinegar with the mustard, and gradually add the olive oil, stirring constantly. The vinaigrette will thicken and combine well. Season to taste with salt and pepper, and add the crushed garlic if used.

EXOTIC SALAD

> **SERVES 4**

250 g (8 oz) bean sprouts
* * *
125 g (4 oz) carrots, grated
* * *
a bunch of watercress, cut into short sprigs
* * *
125 g (4 oz) mooli, sliced finely
* * *
1 lettuce, shredded
* * *
2 kiwi fruit, peeled and sliced finely
* * *
1/4 honeydew melon, peeled and cut into small cubes
* * *
12 lychees, peeled
* * *
175 g (6 oz) seedless grapes
* * *
6–8 tablespoons Garlic Vinaigrette (above)
* * *
PREPARATION TIME: 10–15 MINUTES

This mixture of raw vegetables and exotic fruit dressed with a garlic vinaigrette makes a lunch dish in its own right, perfect for a summer's day served with a basket of crusty, wholemeal bread and a bottle of chilled rosé wine.

Mix the prepared fruit and vegetables together in a large salad bowl. Pour the Garlic Vinaigrette dressing over the salad. Toss the salad well and serve it immediately.

WARM GREEN AND GOLD SALAD

> **SERVES 4–6**

375 g (12 oz) celery hearts, trimmed, or 400 g (13 oz) can celery hearts, drained
* * *
1–2 garlic cloves, peeled and left whole
* * *
150 ml (1/4 pint) white wine
* * *
2 tablespoons lemon juice
* * *
250 g (8 oz) courgettes, sliced
* * *
1 tablespoon Dijon mustard
* * *
1 teaspoon ground turmeric
* * *
4 tablespoons olive oil
* * *
2 yellow peppers, grilled, de-seeded and sliced finely
* * *
2 hard-boiled eggs, quartered
* * *
salt and pepper to taste
* * *
PREPARATION AND COOKING TIME: 30 MINUTES + COOLING

The green is celery hearts and courgettes, the gold is yellow pepper. The green vegetables are cooked in white wine with garlic, the pepper is grilled lightly, then all are tossed in a mixture of mustard and olive oil spiced with turmeric. A perfect lunch dish.

Slice the celery hearts and put into a large saucepan with the garlic, wine and lemon juice. Season to taste with salt. Bring to the boil, cover, and simmer for 7–8 minutes. Add the courgettes, cover again and cook for a further 3 minutes. Drain, reserving the liquid, and leave to cool.

Mix the mustard with the turmeric. Beat in 5 tablespoons of the reserved cooking liquid, then stir in the olive oil. Mix together the celery hearts, courgettes and yellow peppers and put into a serving dish. Season to taste with salt and pepper, and spoon the dressing over the top. Arrange the eggs on top and serve.

FOLLOWING PAGE (CLOCKWISE)
Radish and fennel herb salad
Warm green and gold salad
Exotic salad
Aubergine salad
Spicy bulgar wheat salad
Melting Camembert cookies (PAGE 35)
Vinaigrette

BABY LEEKS IN SPICY WALNUT MAYONNAISE

SERVES 4–6

juice of ¹/₂ lemon

· · ·

1 teaspoon garam masala powder

· · ·

300 ml (¹/₂ pint) Mayonnaise (page 158)

· · ·

2 spring onions, chopped finely

· · ·

75 g (3 oz) shelled walnuts, chopped very finely

· · ·

12 baby leeks, trimmed

· · ·

salt and pepper to taste

· · ·

TO GARNISH

· · ·

chopped walnuts

· · ·

chopped parsley

· · ·

PREPARATION AND COOKING TIME: 10–15 MINUTES + COOLING

A lovely 'salad' for winter, this dish of chilled cooked baby leeks is dressed in a nutty mayonnaise spiced with garam masala, and garnished with a sprinkling of chopped parsley and more chopped walnuts. Serve it with Wholemeal Bread (page 121) or oatcakes.

Add the lemon juice and garam masala to the mayonnaise and mix well. Stir in the spring onions and chopped walnuts and blend thoroughly. Season to taste with salt and pepper.

Cook the leeks in boiling water for about 8–10 minutes until tender. Drain and cool completely. Place in a serving dish and coat with the mayonnaise. Sprinkle with the chopped walnuts and parsley just before serving.

CELERIAC SALAD SPECIAL

SERVES 6

175 g (6 oz) pasta shells

· · ·

1 medium-size celeriac root

· · ·

6 artichoke hearts, sliced

· · ·

175 g (6 oz) button mushrooms, quartered

· · ·

curry paste, to taste

· · ·

300 ml (¹/₂ pint) Mayonnaise (page 158)

· · ·

1 tablespoon finely chopped parsley, to garnish

· · ·

PREPARATION TIME: 25 MINUTES

Celeriac is one of my favourite winter vegetables. It has a delicate but distinctive flavour and makes warming and substantial dishes. This recipe uses raw celeriac and makes a delicious hors d'oeuvre served with fresh bread.

Cook the pasta shells in plenty of boiling water for about 10 minutes, or until cooked through but still firm (*al dente*). Drain thoroughly.

Peel the celeriac and cut it into thin slices. Cut these slices into long julienne strips. Alternatively, shred the peeled vegetable in a food processor. Mix the strips with the artichoke hearts, mushrooms and pasta shells. Mix enough curry paste into the mayonnaise to give it a fairly spicy flavour, and mix it thoroughly with the vegetables and pasta. Chill; then serve the salad sprinkled with the parsley.

Green lettuce rolls
Celeriac salad special
Baby leeks in spicy walnut mayonnaise

RADISH AND FENNEL HERB SALAD

SERVES 4

2 large crisp lettuce hearts, shredded

. . .

1 small bulb of fennel, sliced thinly

. . .

250 g (8 oz) mooli, or ordinary radishes, grated

. . .

4 tablespoons olive oil

. . .

1 tablespoon lemon juice

. . .

a pinch of paprika

. . .

½ small onion, chopped very finely

. . .

3 tablespoons chopped fennel or dill leaves

. . .

PREPARATION TIME: 15 MINUTES

If you can lay your hands on mooli, the long white radish which appears on the shelves in the summer months, do try it in this recipe. Its slight spiciness goes really well with fennel, making an original and refreshing salad.

Mix the lettuce with the fennel and mooli or radishes. Mix the oil with the lemon juice and season with the paprika. Stir in the onion and fennel or dill leaves and toss the salad in this dressing.

NASTURTIUM HARLEQUIN SALAD

SERVES 6–8

18–24 red, yellow and orange nasturtium flowers

. . .

2 heads of radicchio, torn into small pieces

. . .

2 round lettuce hearts, torn into small pieces

. . .

a small bunch of parsley, cut into sprigs

. . .

2 tomatoes, sliced

. . .

1 small onion, cut into fine rings

. . .

125 g (4 oz) black olives

. . .

1 small bulb of fennel, sliced finely

. . .

1 ripe avocado, peeled and stoned

. . .

5 tablespoons Vinaigrette (page 133)

. . .

PREPARATION TIME: 15 MINUTES

This dazzling salad is a conversation-stopper. Many people are shy about serving up flowers with food – and indeed as food – but be brave! Nasturtium flowers are absolutely delicious, soft in texture but slightly spicy in taste, and, of course, their magnificent colours make this salad look wonderful.

Mix the nasturtium flowers with the radicchio and lettuce leaves, and add the parsley, tomatoes, onion, olives and fennel. Cut the avocado flesh into cubes and mix it in. Toss in a liberal quantity of vinaigrette and serve either as a side salad, or as a meal in itself with fresh Granary bread and butter.

PICTURED ON TITLE PAGE

CHAPTER ELEVEN

FESTIVALS AND ENTERTAINING

FOR STARTERS AND SUPPER PARTIES

SAFFRON CAULIFLOWER CHOUX PUFFS

SERVES 6

12 Choux Puffs (page 116)

• • •

FOR THE FILLING

• • •

1 medium-size cauliflower, separated into florets

• • •

150 ml (¼ pint) Béchamel Sauce (page 158)

• • •

4–5 saffron strands

• • •

2 tablespoons warm milk

• • •

salt to taste

• • •

chopped parsley, to garnish

• • •

PREPARATION TIME: 30 MINUTES

Wonderful winter food, these light choux puffs are filled with a purée of cauliflower flavoured with saffron. The crisp golden casing and creamy filling make these a treat, either as an hors d'oeuvre, or as part of a supper table.

Steam the cauliflower over boiling water for about 15 minutes or until tender. Blend the cauliflower and béchamel sauce to a rough purée. Soak the saffron in the milk for 5 minutes; then mix it into the purée and stir thoroughly. Heat through, season to taste with salt, and fill the warm choux puffs with the mixture. Serve as soon as possible sprinkled with chopped parsley.

FOR STARTERS AND SUPPER PARTIES

CRISPY PARCELS OF ASPARAGUS AND DILL

SERVES 4

12 sheets of fillo pastry

• • •

125 g (4 oz) butter or margarine, melted, plus extra for greasing

• • •

dill sprigs, to garnish

• • •

FOR THE FILLING

• • •

500 g (1 lb) asparagus, trimmed

• • •

25 g (1 oz) butter or margarine

• • •

1 onion, chopped finely

• • •

2 garlic cloves, crushed

• • •

125 g (4 oz) cooked basmati rice

• • •

75 g (3 oz) cooked peas

• • •

a large bunch of dill, chopped finely

• • •

salt and pepper to taste

• • •

PREPARATION TIME: ABOUT 30 MINUTES + 25–30 MINUTES COOKING

Inside a crisp, golden-brown parcel of fillo pastry is a mouth-watering filling, soft in texture and with beautiful flavours and aromas. Rice is the soft base for asparagus, peas and fresh dill: a fabulous party dish, either as a starter or as a main course for supper.

Cook the asparagus as instructed (opposite) until it is tender but still firm (*al dente*). Drain; then cut into 1 cm (½-inch) lengths.

To make the filling: heat the butter or margarine in a saucepan, add the onion and garlic and sauté for about 5 minutes, or until soft but not browned. Stir in the rice; then fold in the asparagus, peas and dill. Cook gently for a further 2–3 minutes; then season to taste with salt and pepper.

Preheat the oven to Gas Mark 5/190°C/375°F. Brush 3 sheets of the fillo pastry with melted fat and arrange them one on top of the other, and keeping the remaining sheets covered with a damp tea towel or clingfilm, to prevent drying and cracking. Fold in half crossways and brush with fat again; cut

in half to make two rectangles. Spoon 2–3 tablespoons of the asparagus mixture into the centre of each fillo rectangle, and fold up the short ends to the centre. Then make a parcel by folding the long ends to the centre. Turn the package over carefully so that the seam side is underneath, and place on a large well-greased baking sheet. Repeat with the remaining ingredients to make 8 parcels in total.

Brush with more melted fat and bake for 25–30 minutes, until golden and crisp. Serve garnished with dill sprigs.

ASPARAGUS BÉARNAISE

SERVES 4

1 kg (2 lb) asparagus, trimmed

• • •

3 thin slices of day-old bread, crusts removed

• • •

vegetable oil for frying

• • •

450 ml (¾ pint) Sauce Béarnaise (page 155)

• • •

PREPARATION AND COOKING TIME: 20 MINUTES

Arguably the most epicurean of vegetables, asparagus has been grown and treasured by gourmets for centuries. Serve it with Sauce Béarnaise (page 155) to dip the tips into, and crisp croûtons to accompany it – the Garlic Sesame Croûtons (page 19) are ideal.

Tie the asparagus in bundles and cook, standing it in boiling water halfway up its stalks, so that the tips are steamed rather than boiled. When tender but still slightly crisp (about 5–8 minutes), remove the asparagus from the water, drain, and place on a hot platter.

Meanwhile, cut the bread into tiny triangles, and fry it in vegetable oil until golden on both sides. Drain, and dry on kitchen paper. Keep warm.

Put the asparagus on to warm plates surrounded by the croûtons and hand around the sauce separately.

PICTURED ON PAGE 10

FOR STARTERS AND SUPPER PARTIES

CHAMPIGNONS À LA PROVENÇALE IN FILLO CUPS

> MAKES 12

6 sheets of fillo pastry
. . .
50 g (2 oz) butter or margarine, melted
. . .
500 g (1 lb) mushrooms (shiitake or chestnut mushrooms)
. . .
150 ml (¼ pint) olive oil
. . .
3–4 spring onions, chopped
. . .
2 medium-size garlic cloves, sliced
. . .
juice of ½ lemon
. . .
2 tablespoons chopped parsley
. . .
salt and pepper to taste
. . .

PREPARATION AND COOKING TIME: 35 MINUTES

Light and elegant, these get a special meal off to an original start, and also make an eye-catching addition to a buffet table.

Preheat the oven to Gas Mark 6/200°C/400°F. Brush 3 sheets of fillo pastry with melted fat and place one on top of the other. Cut into 6 squares. Press each square into a well-greased patty tin and crimp up the edges. Repeat with the remaining sheets of fillo. Fill each cup with a ball of crumpled foil, and bake for 10 minutes. Leave to cool on a wire rack.

Remove the stalks from the mushrooms and reserve. Cut the caps into slices. Heat two-thirds of the oil in a frying-pan, add the mushroom caps and sauté for about 5 minutes, or until golden on both sides. Lower the heat, cover and cook gently for 5 minutes. Season to taste. Remove from the heat and keep warm. Chop the mushroom stalks finely. Add the remaining oil to the pan, increase the heat and rapidly cook the chopped mushroom stalks, spring onions and garlic, stirring constantly. Add to the sliced mushrooms. Stir in the lemon juice, sprinkle with the parsley and keep warm.

To assemble, pile the warm mushroom mixture, drained of its juices, into the fillo cups, and serve as soon as possible.

AÏOLI WITH INDONESIAN CRUDITÉS

> SERVES 4–6

FOR THE CRUDITÉS
. . .
cucumber, new potatoes, baby carrots, peppers, french beans, celery, spring onions, mushrooms, cauliflower, tomatoes, mange tout, courgettes, chicory, beetroot
. . .
FOR THE MARINADE
. . .
1 quantity Indonesian Dressing (page 132)
. . .
FOR THE AÏOLI
. . .
2 large garlic cloves, crushed
. . .
450 ml (¾ pint) Mayonnaise (page 158)
. . .

PREPARATION TIME: 20 MINUTES + 24 HOURS MARINATING

This is a great hors d'oeuvre: a strong garlicky mayonnaise served with raw or lightly cooked vegetables to dip into it. It can be made with any selection of vegetables according to season, served with a basket of fresh, warm rolls or oatcakes.

Prepare the vegetables as necessary: wash, peel, top and tail, slice or cut into cubes as appropriate. Vegetables such as new potatoes, french beans, mange tout, cauliflower and courgettes may be lightly steamed and cooled.

Pour the dressing over the vegetables, toss thoroughly, and leave to marinate for 24 hours.

Add the garlic to the mayonnaise. Leave in a cool place until ready to serve.

Strain just before serving, and arrange the crudités decoratively on a platter.

PREVIOUS PAGE (CLOCKWISE)
Steamboat
Spice-island casserole
Indian puris (PAGE 121)
Aïoli with Indonesian crudités
Malay-style gourmet platter
Teriyaki sauce (PAGE 153)
Satay sauce (PAGE 152)
Sweet and sour sauce (PAGE 155)
Sauce verte (PAGE 157)

FESTIVE MEALS

HOT MUSHROOM TERRINE

> SERVES 4

500 g (1 lb) button mushrooms
· · ·
4 eggs
· · ·
125 g (4 oz) fresh breadcrumbs
· · ·
75 g (3 oz) vegetarian Cheddar cheese, grated finely
· · ·
a small bunch of basil
· · ·
6 tablespoons olive oil
· · ·
3 garlic cloves, crushed
· · ·
1 tablespoon soy sauce
· · ·
2 tablespoons chopped parsley
· · ·
75 g (3 oz) nibbed almonds, toasted
· · ·
salt and pepper to taste
· · ·

PREPARATION TIME: 35 MINUTES + 1 HOUR COOKING + 10 MINUTES STANDING

Sensational in flavour as well as texture, a slice of this wonderful mushroom loaf makes a memorable starter at any time of the year. It is delicious hot, warm or cold, so can also be offered as part of a buffet meal.

Blend or finely chop the mushrooms, and set aside.

Preheat the oven to Gas Mark 6/200°C/400°F. Blend all the remaining ingredients, except the nibbed almonds, to a purée. Fold in the mushrooms and the nibbed almonds. Season to taste with salt and pepper. Pour into a lightly greased 20 × 13 × 9 cm (8 × 5 × 3½-inch) loaf tin. Bake for 20 minutes; then lower the oven temperature to Gas Mark 4/180°C/350°F and cook for a further 40 minutes, or until a sharp knife inserted into the centre of the terrine comes out clean.

Leave the terrine to stand for 10 minutes on a wire rack, covered with a tea towel, then turn it out. Serve cut into thick slices.

MALAY-STYLE GOURMET PLATTER

> SERVES 6

This combination of four delicious dishes makes a real feast of delicate morsels. I like to arrange them on the table intermingled with plates of lightly steamed cold vegetables such as courgettes, french beans and mange tout. Add a couple of dipping sauces (pages 152–158), and then a basket of mixed breads, including Indian Puris (page 121), is the only other requirement.

ARTICHOKE HEARTS WITH PURÉE ST GERMAIN
· · ·
6 medium-size globe artichokes, cooked and cooled
· · ·
250 g (8 oz) cooked peas
· · ·
2 tablespoons mixed herbs, chopped
· · ·
2 tablespoons Béchamel Sauce (page 158) or soured cream
· · ·
salt and pepper to taste
· · ·

PREPARATION TIME: 55 MINUTES

Prise apart the leaves of each artichoke to reveal the soft central leaves and dry, fibrous 'choke'. Scrape this out with a teaspoon and rinse in cold water. Repeat with the remaining artichokes. Trim the stem and the base of each artichoke so that it will stand upright.

Purée the peas with the herbs and béchamel sauce or soured cream and season to taste with salt and pepper. Fill the artichokes with the mixture.

LITTLE TOMATO AND CARROT PASTRIES
· · ·
2 quantities Shortcrust Pastry (page 34)
· · ·
4 medium-size tomatoes, skinned and chopped
· · ·
250 g (8 oz) baby carrots, cooked
· · ·
2 tablespoons thick-set natural yogurt
· · ·
salt, pepper and nutmeg
· · ·

PREPARATION TIME: 30 MINUTES

Make the pastry as instructed (page 34) and use it to make 12 small pastry shells, baked blind (page 34).

FESTIVE MEALS

Purée the tomatoes and carrots with the yogurt and season to taste with salt, pepper and nutmeg. Pile into the pastry shells and serve as soon as possible.

STUFFED MUSHROOMS
. . .
250 g (8 oz) asparagus
. . .
12 flat mushrooms, stalks removed
. . .
250 g (8 oz) cottage cheese, puréed
. . .
25 g (1 oz) flaked almonds, toasted
. . .
PREPARATION TIME: 15–20 MINUTES

Cook the asparagus as instructed (page 140) until tender but still firm (*al dente*). Drain.

Steam the mushrooms for 2–3 minutes, until tender but not limp. Chop the asparagus into 1 cm (½-inch) lengths and fold into the puréed cottage cheese. Spoon the mixture into the mushroom caps and sprinkle with the almonds.

COLD SPICY NOODLES SATAY
. . .
300 g (10 oz) Chinese egg noodles, soaked in hot water
. . .
5 tablespoons Satay Sauce (page 152)
. . .
3 spring onions, chopped finely
. . .
PREPARATION TIME: 5–10 MINUTES + COOLING

Drain the prepared noodles and, while still warm, toss them in the satay sauce, and then allow to cool. Serve sprinkled with the spring onions.

SPICE-ISLAND CASSEROLE

SERVES 4–6

3 tablespoons desiccated coconut
. . .
750 ml (1¼ pints) boiling water
. . .
4 tablespoons vegetable oil
. . .
8 spring onions, chopped
. . .
250 g (8 oz) oyster or button mushrooms, sliced
. . .
175 g (6 oz) chinese leaves, shredded
. . .
175 g (6 oz) small french beans
. . .
175 g (6 oz) mange tout
. . .
1 small mooli, sliced finely
. . .
125 g (4 oz) fresh pineapple, cut into cubes
. . .
3 teaspoons Chinese 5-spice powder
. . .
½ chilli, de-seeded
. . .
125 g (4 oz) dry-roasted peanuts, ground coarsely
. . .
PREPARATION AND COOKING TIME: 25–30 MINUTES + STANDING

A steaming casserole of crisp vegetables is cooked in coconut milk with chilli and Chinese 5-spice powder – flavours evocative of Indonesian cuisine. It makes a really delicious and unusual main course, served with rice and Indian Puris (page 121). Serve with a tossed side salad of cos lettuce, watercress and sliced radishes.

Infuse the coconut in the hot water for 10 minutes.

Meanwhile, heat the oil, add the spring onions and mushrooms, and sauté for 2–3 minutes. Then stir in all the remaining vegetables and the pineapple, and toss together until well coated and beginning to heat through.

Strain off the coconut milk and blend it to a creamy consistency with the 5-spice, chilli and peanuts. Pour the sauce over the vegetables. Simmer for 5–8 minutes, until they are all cooked through but still slightly crisp. Leave the casserole to stand for a while before serving – or leave it until the next day and reheat gently: the flavours develop beautifully.

FESTIVE MEALS

STEAMBOAT

SERVES 6

FOR THE STOCK

• • •

1.2 litres (2 pints) vegetable stock

• • •

2 garlic cloves, sliced

• • •

2.5 cm (1-inch) piece of root ginger, peeled and grated finely

• • •

5 spring onions, sliced finely

FOR THE RAW INGREDIENTS

• • •

1.25 kg (3 lb) mixed vegetables, such as chinese leaves, celery, okra, mange tout, baby sweetcorn, courgettes, asparagus, yellow peppers – all trimmed as necessary, and sliced or diced where appropriate

• • •

FOR THE DIPPING SAUCES

• • •

A choice of Hollandaise, Satay, Escargot Butter, Poivre-vert, Beurre Noisette, Sauce Verte, Sweet and Sour (pages 152–158)

• • •

PREPARATION AND COOKING TIME: 10–15 MINUTES

'Steamboat' is an elegant and epicurean fondue – vegetarian style! A selection of colourful and exotic vegetables are arranged around a fondue pot of aromatic stock, dipped into it until lightly cooked, and then eaten with a choice of sauces. Serve this meal with rice, a tossed mixed salad and fresh home-made bread (page 121). The Chapatis (page 120) go down a treat, too.

Put the stock into a saucepan and add the garlic, ginger and spring onions. Simmer gently for 10 minutes; then strain into a fondue pot and simmer gently over a low burner.

Arrange the vegetables decoratively on a platter. Skewer them on to kebab sticks and dip them into the simmering stock, until lightly cooked. To eat them, remove from the skewer (which will be very hot) and, with a fork, dip them into the sauces of your choice.

CHRISTMAS

VEGETABLE STEW WITH WINE AND HERBS

SERVES 6

5 tablespoons vegetable oil

• • •

3 medium-size courgettes, cut into thick slices

• • •

250 g (8 oz) small carrots, cut lengthways

• • •

500 g (1 lb) new potatoes, scrubbed and diced if necessary

• • •

2 leeks, sliced

• • •

500 g (1 lb) small button mushrooms

• • •

1 parsnip, peeled and sliced

• • •

1 head of celery, washed and sliced

• • •

2 bay leaves

• • •

3 tablespoons plain wholemeal flour

• • •

450 ml (3/4 pint) red wine

• • •

12 shallots or small onions

• • •

3 teaspoons dried thyme

• • •

175 g (6 oz) goat cheese or Brie

• • •

salt to taste

• • •

PREPARATION TIME: 20 MINUTES + 1¼–1½ HOURS COOKING

An ideal dish for a winter dinner party, this is reminiscent of boeuf bourguignon *– but without the beef, of course.*

Heat the oil in a large flameproof casserole dish, add the vegetables and bay leaves, and sauté gently for 20 minutes. Sprinkle over the flour and mix in well. Pour in the wine and stir until smooth. Add the shallots and thyme and cover.

Preheat the oven to Gas Mark 2/150°C/300°F. Bake the stew for 50 minutes; alternatively simmer the casserole on top of the stove for 1 hour. In either case the vegetables should be tender but not too soft.

Just before serving, remove the bay leaves, and slice or grate the cheese and scatter it over the top of the stew. Grill until the cheese browns and bubbles; serve immediately.

CHRISTMAS

ARCHANGEL ROAST

SERVES 6–8

125 ml (4 fl oz) olive oil, plus extra for greasing
· · ·
2 medium-size onions, chopped
· · ·
2 garlic cloves, crushed
· · ·
3 leeks, sliced
· · ·
½ head of celery, sliced
· · ·
250 g (8 oz) cooked peas
· · ·
375 g (12 oz) fresh wholemeal breadcrumbs
· · ·
175 g (6 oz) cheese, grated
· · ·
4 eggs, beaten
· · ·
1–2 tablespoons soy sauce
· · ·
4 courgettes, cut into small cubes
· · ·
4 tomatoes, chopped
· · ·
1 teaspoon dried basil
· · ·
1 teaspoon dried thyme
· · ·

PREPARATION TIME: 40–50 MINUTES + 45–50 MINUTES COOKING
+ 20 MINUTES STANDING

A festive loaf, made with winter vegetables such as celery and leeks, this is filled with a layer of courgettes, tomatoes and onions cooked with herbs. Perfect Christmas fare, it makes a special meal that is best served with all the trimmings – brussels sprouts, roast potatoes, bread sauce and cranberry jelly.

In a large flameproof casserole dish, heat 5 tablespoons of the oil, add half the chopped onion, the garlic, leeks and celery, and sauté, stirring constantly, for about 5 minutes, or until they begin to soften and are well coated in the oil. Cover the pan and cook gently for 20 minutes. Stir in the peas, and remove the mixture from the heat. Add the breadcrumbs, cheese, eggs and soy sauce, and mix well.

For the filling, heat the remaining oil in a saucepan, add the courgettes, tomatoes, herbs and the remaining chopped onion, and sauté, stirring, for 3–4 minutes. Cover the casserole dish and cook gently for 15–20 minutes, stirring occasionally, until the mixture forms a thick sauce.

Preheat the oven to Gas Mark 3/160°C/325°F. Oil a 2.25-litre (4-pint) loaf tin, press in half the roast mix, and cover with the filling. Top with the remaining roast mixture, and bake for 45–50 minutes. Cool the roast on a wire rack for 20 minutes before turning it out.

CHRISTMAS CROÛTE

SERVES 6–8

FOR THE NUT PASTRY
· · ·
175 g (6 oz) butter or margarine
· · ·
250 g (8 oz) plain flour
· · ·
50 g (2 oz) plain wholemeal flour
· · ·
75 g (3 oz) shelled walnuts, chopped
· · ·
5 tablespoons cold water
FOR THE FILLING
· · ·
40 g (1½ oz) butter or margarine
· · ·
1 onion, sliced
· · ·
1 red pepper, cut in strips
· · ·
2 small fennel bulbs, sliced thinly
· · ·
250 g (8 oz) courgettes, diced
· · ·
125 ml (4 fl oz) white wine
· · ·
250 g (8 oz) cream cheese
· · ·
2 tomatoes, chopped
· · ·
juice of 1 lemon
· · ·
250 g (8 oz) cooked basmati rice
· · ·
3 hard-boiled eggs, chopped
· · ·
salt and pepper to taste
· · ·
1 egg, beaten
· · ·
sesame seeds, to garnish
· · ·

PREPARATION TIME: 30–40 MINUTES + 20 MINUTES CHILLING + 50 MINUTES COOKING
+ 10 MINUTES STANDING

CHRISTMAS

A great centrepiece for a Christmas meal, this looks sensational, and the flavours and textures are wonderful. A real treat served with brussels sprouts, a gratin of leeks and roast potatoes.

Blend all the pastry ingredients together until smooth. Cover and chill for about 20 minutes before use.

Melt the butter or margarine in a large saucepan, add the onion, pepper, fennel and courgettes, and sauté for 3–4 minutes, or until the vegetables have softened. Add the wine, and simmer for 8–10 minutes. Cover the pan, remove from the heat and leave to cool.

Mix together the cream cheese, tomatoes, lemon juice, rice, and eggs. Add to the cooled fennel mixture and season to taste with salt and pepper.

Preheat the oven to Gas Mark 4/180°C/350°F. Roll out the pastry into a large, long rectangle. Grease a baking sheet and carefully lift the pastry onto it, leaving plenty hanging over the edges. Pile the filling into the middle of the pastry, cut the uncovered pastry into 2.5 cm (1-inch) strips, fold each strip over the centre of the filling, and press together. Tuck in the ends. Brush with the beaten egg and scatter with sesame seeds. Bake for 50 minutes. Cool on a wire rack for 10 minutes before serving.

EASTER

SURPRISE EASTER EGGS

SERVES 6

2 large aubergines
· · ·
olive oil for greasing
· · ·
50 g (2 oz) butter or margarine
· · ·
250 g (8 oz) cooked spinach
· · ·
2 eggs
· · ·
1 small nutmeg, grated
· · ·
250 g (8 oz) feta cheese
· · ·
250 g (8 oz) cottage cheese
· · ·
1 large garlic clove, crushed
· · ·
a large bunch of parsley, chopped finely
· · ·
10 felafels
· · ·
salt and pepper to taste
· · ·

PREPARATION TIME: 30 MINUTES + 15–20 MINUTES COOKING

These amazing morsels take time to prepare, but your efforts will be rewarded. These are something really special, and quite different.

Preheat the oven to Gas Mark 3/160°C/325°F. Slice the top and stem off the aubergines, and cut into 5 mm (¼-inch) slices (about 20 slices in total); discard the outer ones which will be mostly skin. Liberally oil enough baking sheets to arrange the aubergine slices without overlapping. Brush the slices with more oil and bake for 20 minutes, turning after 10 minutes, until tender but not too soft. Leave to cool.

Melt the fat, add the spinach and sauté for 1–2 minutes. Purée with the eggs and nutmeg. Add the cheeses, garlic and seasonings, and purée again. Stir in the parsley and cool.

Turn the oven up to Gas Mark 4/180°C/350°F. Cut each felafel in half, spread the filling evenly over the baked aubergine slices and place half a felafel in the centre of each. Curl the slices around it and secure each one with a cocktail stick. Stand the finished egg rolls upright in a liberally oiled shallow ovenproof dish and cover loosely with foil. Bake for about 15–20 minutes, until heated through.

EASTER

NUTTY CROUSTADE OF PALE GREEN VEGETABLES

> SERVES 4–6

1½ medium-size cauliflowers, cut into florets
• • •
2 medium-size fennel bulbs, chopped
• • •
15 g (½ oz) butter or margarine
• • •
1 onion, chopped
• • •
1 teaspoon dried thyme
• • •
1 bay leaf
• • •
200 ml (7 fl oz) white wine
• • •
284 ml (½ pint) carton of single cream
• • •
1 teaspoon Chinese 5-spice powder
• • •
3 tablespoons chopped fennel or dill leaves
• • •
125 g (4 oz) pine kernels
• • •
150 g (5 oz) dried breadcrumbs
• • •
walnut or sunflower oil
• • •
salt and pepper to taste
• • •
PREPARATION TIME: 25 MINUTES + 30 MINUTES COOKING

A great favourite of mine, this pale green mixture of vegetables, lightly flavoured with the first fresh fennel of the spring, is topped with a golden, nutty mixture of crisp breadcrumbs and pine kernels. A delectable centrepiece for an Easter meal, alongside buttery new potatoes, and a selection of lightly steamed spring vegetables.

Steam the cauliflower and the fennel over boiling water for about 15 minutes, or until they are cooked through but still firm (*al dente*). Heat the butter or margarine in a saucepan, add the onion, thyme and bay leaf, and sauté until the onion is softened. Add the wine, cover the pan and simmer for 10 minutes. Add the cream, 5-spice and chopped fennel or dill leaves. Season to taste with salt and pepper. Transfer the mixture to an ovenproof dish with the cauliflower and fennel and remove the bay leaf.

Preheat the oven to Gas Mark 4/180°C/350°F. Combine the pine kernels with the breadcrumbs, salt and enough oil to thoroughly moisten the mixture. Spread this over the cauliflower. Bake for 30 minutes, until the topping is golden and crisp.

Champignons à la Provençale in fillo cups
Vodka and green peppercorn sauce (PAGE 154)
Christmas croûte
Vegetable stew with wine and herbs
Archangel roast

CHAPTER TWELVE

CLASSIC SAUCES

Many of the great classic sauces from world cuisines were originally designed to accompany meat or fish, but since many of them are themselves vegetarian, it seems appropriate to include them in vegetarian cooking. Beautiful sauces are an important part of the cook's art, and can transform very simple meals into memorable occasions. All the following sauces serve four people.

SAUCE POIVRE-VERT

50 g (2 oz) butter or margarine
· · ·
25 g (1 oz) bottled green peppercorns, drained and crushed well
· · ·
142 ml (¼ pint) carton of single cream
· · ·
150 ml (¼ pint) skimmed milk
· · ·
PREPARATION AND COOKING TIME: 5–10 MINUTES

A lovely sauce for steamed spring vegetables, and with new potatoes. It is delicious with Soft Vegetable Rice Chinese-style (page 101).

Melt the fat in a saucepan, add the peppercorns and simmer for 2 minutes. Stir in the cream and milk and cook for 1–2 minutes.

PICTURED ON PAGE 102

SATAY SAUCE

2 tablespoons desiccated coconut
· · ·
300 ml (½ pint) boiling water
· · ·
2 dried chillies, soaked in warm water
· · ·
1 stalk of chopped lemon grass, or 2 teaspoons grated lemon zest
· · ·
2.5 cm (1-inch) piece of root ginger, peeled and grated
· · ·
1 vegetable stock cube, crumbled
· · ·
125 g (4 oz) dry-roasted peanuts, ground coarsely
· · ·
2 tablespoons vegetable oil
· · ·
1 tablespoon sugar
· · ·
salt to taste
· · ·
PREPARATION AND COOKING TIME: 15 MINUTES + COOLING

This Malaysian sauce makes a delectable addition to Steamboat (page 147), and is excellent with Steamed Tamari Mushrooms (page 86).

Put the coconut into a jug and cover with the boiling water. Leave it to stand for 10 minutes, then strain it.

Blend the chillies, lemon grass, ginger, stock cube and peanuts and fry in the oil for 4–5 minutes. Add the coconut milk and sugar and season. Stir over a gentle heat for 5 minutes; then cool. Store in an airtight jar in the refrigerator.

PICTURED ON PAGE 142

ESCARGOT BUTTER

125 g (4 oz) butter or margarine

• • •

a large bunch of parsley, chopped finely

• • •

2–3 large garlic cloves, crushed

• • •

salt and pepper to taste

PREPARATION AND COOKING TIME: 10–15 MINUTES

The classic French butter, this is excellent with lightly steamed courgettes or french beans; as a dipping sauce for Steamboat (page 147); and with Oeufs Pochés sur Champignons (page 32).

Melt the butter or margarine in a saucepan, add the parsley and simmer gently for 5 minutes, stirring frequently. Add the garlic and simmer for a further 5 minutes. Season to taste.

You can also make the consistency thinner using a little cream for a sauce rather than a butter.

PICTURED ON PAGE 37

SAUCE HOLLANDAISE

3 tablespoons white wine vinegar

• • •

2 tablespoons cold water

• • •

3 egg yolks, beaten

• • •

175 g (6 oz) unsalted butter, warmed

• • •

salt, pepper and lemon juice to taste

PREPARATION AND COOKING TIME: 10–15 MINUTES

An elegant sauce for spring and summer vegetables, this also goes well with fritters and beignets, and is delightful with Kibbeh (page 108).

Place the vinegar and water in a saucepan and reduce to 1 tablespoon of liquid by boiling hard. Put into a bowl and place it above a saucepan of water over a low heat. Add the egg yolks and stir thoroughly, and then gradually stir in the butter, a little at a time. Stir constantly: if the sauce thickens too quickly add a few drops of cold water. Do not allow it to overheat. Season to taste with salt, pepper and lemon juice.

PICTURED ON PAGE 61

SAUCE PRINTANIER

125 g (4 oz) peas, cooked

• • •

125 g (4 oz) asparagus, cooked

• • •

75 g (3 oz) butter or margarine, melted

• • •

5 tablespoons Béchamel Sauce (page 158) or soured cream

• • •

a little single cream

• • •

salt and pepper to taste

PREPARATION TIME: 20–30 MINUTES

Lovely with mange tout, and with Aubergines Frites aux Fines Herbs (page 81).

Liquidise the vegetables with the melted butter or margarine and the béchamel sauce or soured cream. Thin it out with a little cream and season to taste with salt and pepper if necessary.

PICTURED ON PAGE 83

TERIYAKI SAUCE

5 tablespoons soy sauce

• • •

3 tablespoons white wine

• • •

3 tablespoons brown sugar

• • •

1 teaspoon grated root ginger

• • •

2 garlic cloves, crushed

• • •

1 tablespoon sesame oil

• • •

1/4 teaspoon mustard powder

• • •

PREPARATION TIME: 5 MINUTES + 30 MINUTES STANDING

This classic Japanese sauce is one of the best of the dipping sauces for Steamboat (page 147), and is also excellent with fritters – especially Mushroom Butterflies (page 45), and Okra Beignets (page 44).

Mix all the ingredients together well and leave to stand for 30 minutes before using.

PICTURED ON PAGE 142

SAUCE FINES HERBES

25 g (1 oz) butter or margarine

* * *

2 shallots or small onions, chopped very finely

* * *

5 tablespoons white wine

* * *

300 ml (½ pint) Béchamel Sauce (page 158)

* * *

3–4 tablespoons vegetable stock or milk

* * *

1 tablespoon chopped parsley

* * *

1 tablespoon chopped chervil

* * *

1 tablespoon chopped tarragon

* * *

salt, pepper and lemon juice to taste

* * *

PREPARATION AND COOKING TIME: 20 MINUTES

Delectable with Celery and Nut Roast (page 68), with September Stuffed Courgettes (page 65), and with Vegetable Terrine (page 72).

Melt the butter or margarine in a saucepan, add the shallots or onions, and stir them until they soften a little. Stir in the wine and reduce the liquid over a fairly high heat for 5 minutes. Add the béchamel sauce and mix well; then thin the sauce with stock or milk. Stir in the herbs and cook for 5 minutes. Season to taste with salt, pepper and lemon juice.

PICTURED ON PAGE 71

SAUCE DIJONNAISE

300 ml (½ pint) Béchamel Sauce (page 158)

* * *

2 tablespoons coarse-grain mustard

* * *

50 g (2 oz) Gruyère or medium-hard cheese, grated

* * *

salt and pepper to taste

* * *

PREPARATION AND COOKING TIME: 10 MINUTES

Delicious with Puff-pastry Triangles (page 114), you can also try this with Stuffed Cabbage Leaves (page 65).

Heat the béchamel sauce and stir in the mustard. Mix well, add the cheese, and cook until it melts. Season to taste.

PICTURED ON PAGE 123

SAUCE CRESSONNIÈRE

a bunch of watercress, chopped finely

* * *

5 tablespoons olive oil

* * *

1 tablespoon tarragon vinegar

* * *

2 hard-boiled egg yolks

* * *

150 ml (¼ pint) Mayonnaise (page 158)

* * *

PREPARATION TIME: 10 MINUTES

A beautiful green sauce which enhances the delicate flavours of Vegetable Terrine (page 72), completes the Millet Pilav (page 108), and makes a meal out of the Spicy Mushroom Pakoras (page 42).

Liquidise the watercress with the other ingredients until it makes a smooth sauce. Serve cold.

PICTURED ON PAGE 109

VODKA AND GREEN PEPPERCORN SAUCE

40 g (1½ oz) butter or margarine

* * *

15 g (½ oz) bottled green peppercorns, drained and crushed

* * *

2–3 tablespoons vodka

* * *

142 ml (¼ pint) carton of double cream

* * *

PREPARATION AND COOKING TIME: ABOUT 10 MINUTES

This sauce is unbelievably good with french beans or lightly steamed courgettes. It is also a treat with Archangel Roast (page 148) or Christmas Croûte (page 148), and is an elegant sauce to accompany the Crispy Parcels of Asparagus and Dill (page 140).

In a small saucepan melt the butter or margarine and heat until it sizzles. Stir in the peppercorns and cook for 2–3 minutes; then add the vodka. Lower the heat a little, and stir in the cream gradually so that it blends with the green peppercorn mixture. Serve hot.

PICTURED ON PAGE 150

SWEET AND SOUR SAUCE

3 garlic cloves, crushed

· · ·

2 tablespoons soft brown sugar

· · ·

2 tablespoons cider vinegar

· · ·

1 tablespoon soy sauce

· · ·

1 tablespoon tomato purée

· · ·

125 ml (4 fl oz) water

· · ·

½ teaspoon cornflour (optional)

· · ·

PREPARATION AND COOKING TIME: 10–15 MINUTES

This is excellent with Stuffed Cabbage Leaves (page 65).

Mix all the ingredients in a pan and stir until the sugar has dissolved. Simmer gently for 10–15 minutes. Add more soy sauce to taste if desired, or ½ teaspoon cornflour dissolved in 2 teaspoons cold water if you prefer a thicker sauce.

PICTURED ON PAGES 66 AND 143

TOMATO AND ORANGE SAUCE

1 onion, chopped

· · ·

2 garlic cloves, crushed

· · ·

397 g (14 oz) can of tomatoes

· · ·

2 tablespoons chopped oregano

· · ·

juice and zest of 1 orange

· · ·

a pinch of sugar

· · ·

salt and pepper to taste

· · ·

PREPARATION AND COOKING TIME: 15 MINUTES

Delicious with Lentil and Mushroom Slice (page 101), and excellent with Christmas Croûte (page 148).

Blend all the ingredients until smooth. Heat gently for 10 minutes; check the seasoning, adding more sugar if wished.

PICTURED ON PAGE 106

SAUCE BÉARNAISE

5 tablespoons white wine

· · ·

2 tablespoons tarragon vinegar

· · ·

2 shallots or small onions, chopped finely

· · ·

125 g (4 oz) butter or margarine, cut into small pieces

· · ·

3 egg yolks, beaten

· · ·

a small bunch of tarragon, chopped finely

· · ·

salt, pepper and lemon juice to taste

· · ·

PREPARATION AND COOKING TIME: 35 MINUTES + 10 MINUTES STANDING

This elegant French sauce goes beautifully with Vegetable Mille-Feuilles (page 117), and is unbeatable with Vegetable Terrine (page 72). It is sensational with steamed broccoli, courgettes or spinach.

Boil the white wine, vinegar and shallots or onions with a little black pepper in a saucepan until the liquid is reduced to about 2 tablespoons. Add a few drops of cold water, and pour this mixture into a bowl. Place it above a saucepan of water over a low heat. Gradually add the butter or margarine, stirring constantly over the heat, adding more fat as each portion melts. Then stir in the beaten egg yolks, mixing them together carefully until the sauce thickens, being careful not to let it overheat. Stir in the tarragon, season to taste with salt and lemon juice and remove from the heat. Leave the sauce to stand for 10 minutes before serving.

Make this with mint instead of tarragon and you have a *Sauce Paloise.*

PICTURED ON PAGE 10

BEURRE NOISETTE

75 g (3 oz) butter or margarine

· · ·

2 tablespoons white wine vinegar

· · ·

PREPARATION AND COOKING TIME: 5 MINUTES

So simple to make, this is delightful with french beans, new potatoes or baby carrots, and is one of the best sauces for courgettes in the summer.

Melt the butter or margarine in a saucepan and heat it until it sizzles and turns nut-brown. Pour in the vinegar and leave it to froth for a minute or so before pouring the sauce over the vegetables of your choice.

BEURRE BLANC

3 shallots or small onions, chopped very finely

• • •

3 tablespoons white wine vinegar

• • •

3 tablespoons white wine

• • •

175 g (6 oz) unsalted butter or margarine

PREPARATION AND COOKING TIME: 25 MINUTES

This is brilliant with new potatoes, and fantastic with spinach.

Simmer the shallots or onions in the vinegar and white wine until they are completely soft, and the liquid has been reduced. Leave it to cool a little, then start adding the butter or margarine, about 25 g (1 oz) at a time. Stir constantly over a gentle heat until the sauce is thick and creamy.

SAUCE VERTE

a large bunch of chervil, chopped

• • •

50 g (2 oz) watercress

• • •

300 ml (½ pint) Mayonnaise (page 158)

• • •

3 tablespoons cooked spinach

• • •

salt to taste

• • •

PREPARATION AND COOKING TIME: 10 MINUTES

A lovely summer sauce for cooked vegetables, hot or cold, and crudités.

Steam the chervil with the watercress for 1–2 minutes; allow to cool. Purée all the remaining ingredients together to give a smooth, green sauce. Season to taste with salt.

PICTURED ON PAGE 142

Walnut sauce from Georgia
Beurre blanc
Sauce ravigote
Sauce verte
Beurre noisette

WALNUT SAUCE FROM GEORGIA

1 tablespoon very finely chopped onion

• • •

75 g (3 oz) shelled walnuts, chopped

• • •

1 garlic clove, crushed

• • •

1 tablespoon white wine vinegar

• • •

142 ml (¼ pint) carton of single or soured cream

• • •

salt to taste

• • •

PREPARATION TIME: 10–15 MINUTES

A cold sauce which is lovely with french or runner beans, and on spinach. Try it with Aubergine Frites aux Fines Herbes (page 81), and with any of the fritters and beignets.

Put the onions, walnuts and garlic into a small bowl and blend to a paste. Stir in the vinegar, purée the mixture again, and season to taste with salt. Thin the sauce with single or soured cream, and check the seasoning.

SAUCE RAVIGOTE

4 tablespoons olive oil

• • •

1 tablespoon white wine vinegar

• • •

1–2 teaspoons capers, chopped very finely

• • •

a small bunch of fines herbes, chopped very finely

• • •

1 teaspoon Dijon mustard

• • •

25 g (1 oz) shallots or small onions, chopped very finely

• • •

a pinch of sugar

• • •

PREPARATION TIME: 10 MINUTES + 30 MINUTES STANDING

A delicious salad dressing, and wonderful with cold cooked vegetables.

Mix the oil with the vinegar and stir in the remaining ingredients. Leave the sauce to stand for at least 30 minutes before serving.

SAUCE NORMANDE

40 g (1½ oz) butter or margarine

• • •

250 g (8 oz) mushrooms, chopped

• • •

300 ml (½ pint) Béchamel Sauce (below)

• • •

a little cream

• • •

salt and pepper to taste

• • •

PREPARATION AND COOKING TIME: ABOUT 20 MINUTES

*T*his goes perfectly with Cheesy Courgette Strudel (page 113); with Archangel Roast (page 148); and with Lentil and Mushroom Slice (page 101).

Melt the butter or margarine in a saucepan, add the mushrooms, and cook for 8–10 minutes, or until very soft. Stir the mushrooms and their juices into the béchamel sauce. Liquidise to a fine purée and season to taste with salt and pepper. Thin out with a little cream if necessary.

PICTURED ON PAGE 118

BERGAMOT MAYONNAISE

MAKES 300 ML (½ PINT)

25 g (1 oz) butter or margarine

• • •

2 shallots or small onions, chopped finely

• • •

2 tablespoons white wine

• • •

3 tablespoons finely chopped bergamot leaves

• • •

300 ml (½ pint) Mayonnaise (above)

• • •

salt and pepper to taste

• • •

PREPARATION TIME: 20 MINUTES + COOLING

*U*se this mayonnaise for summery salads of your choice: the addition of wine, along with the unusual taste of bergamot, makes it a dressing with a difference. Try it with sage instead of bergamot, too.

Melt the butter or margarine in a saucepan, add the shallots or onions and cook them over a very gentle heat for 5–10 minutes, stirring frequently. Add the wine and cook for 3–4 minutes. Stir in the bergamot and simmer for 3–4 minutes until the leaves are softened and fragrant; then cool. Stir into the mayonnaise, and season to taste.

MAYONNAISE

MAKES 300 ML (½ PINT)

1 egg

• • •

1 teaspoon mustard powder

• • •

300 ml (½ pint) sunflower or olive oil

• • •

salt and pepper to taste

• • •

PREPARATION TIME: 5 MINUTES

Break the egg into a food processor and add the mustard, salt and pepper. Start to work the processor and gradually pour in a thin stream of oil. Stop pouring from time to time to let the mixture thicken – and be careful not to pour too fast right at the beginning otherwise the mixture will separate. Check the seasoning, and refrigerate until ready to use.

Alternatively, if you're not using a food processor, beat the egg a little with a wooden spoon and begin to pour in the oil, drop by drop, stirring constantly. Stir vigorously until the mixture starts to thicken, increasing the oil flow to a thin stream. Check the seasoning and refrigerate until ready to use.

BÉCHAMEL SAUCE

40 g (1½ oz) butter or margarine

• • •

25 g (1 oz) plain flour = 1 heaped dessert spoon

300 ml (½ pint) warm milk

• • •

salt, pepper and a pinch of nutmeg to taste

• • •

PREPARATION AND COOKING TIME: 10–15 MINUTES

The quickest way to make béchamel sauce is to melt the butter in a small, heavy saucepan. Gradually stir in the flour, using a wooden spoon. Add the milk slowly, stirring constantly until the sauce thickens. Season to taste with the salt, pepper and nutmeg and simmer over a very low heat for 5–6 minutes.

The traditional way to make béchamel sauce is to place the milk, salt, pepper and nutmeg in a saucepan and bring it slowly to the boil. Remove from the heat, cover the pan and allow the flavours to infuse for 15 minutes. In a clean heavy-based pan, melt the butter, stir in the flour, and cook for 1–2 minutes. Gradually add the infused milk a little at a time and bring to the boil, stirring continuously, for 5–6 minutes.

INDEX TO RECIPES